Jocelyn B

Jocelyn Bioh: Three Plays

Merry Wives
Nollywood Dreams
School Girls; Or, The African Mean Girls Play

JOCELYN BIOH

methuen | drama
LONDON • NEW YORK • OXFORD • NEW DELHI • SYDNEY

METHUEN DRAMA
Bloomsbury Publishing Plc
50 Bedford Square, London, WC1B 3DP, UK
1385 Broadway, New York, NY 10018, USA
29 Earlsfort Terrace, Dublin 2, Ireland

BLOOMSBURY, METHUEN DRAMA and the Methuen Drama logo are trademarks
of Bloomsbury Publishing Plc

First published in Great Britain 2024
School Girls; Or, The African Mean Girls Play first published
by Bloomsbury Methuen Drama 2023

A catalogue record for this book is available from the British Library.

A catalog record for this book is available from the Library of Congress.

ISBN: PB: 978-1-3504-2334-3
       ePDF: 978-1-3504-2336-7
       eBook: 978-1-3504-2335-0

Series: Methuen Drama Play Collections

Typeset by RefineCatch Limited, Bungay, Suffolk
Printed and bound in Great Britain

To find out more about our authors and books visit www.bloomsbury.com
and sign up for our newsletters.

Contents

Merry Wives

Originally Developed by
The Public Theater
Oskar Eustis, Artistic Director
Patrick Willingham, Executive Director

Merry Wives was originally developed by the Public Theater (Oskar Eustis, Artistic Director; Patrick Willingham, Executive Director) on July 27, 2021 in New York City. It was directed by Saheem Ali, the scenic design was by Beowulf Boritt, the costume design was by Dede Ayite, the hair, wig, and makeup design was by Cookie Jordan, the lighting design was by Jiyoun Chang, the sound design was by Kai Harada and Palmer Hefferan, the original music was by Michael Thurber, the original drum compositions were by Farai Malianga, the fight direction was by Rocío Mendez, the choreography was by Darrell Grand Moultrie, and the production stage manager was Narda E. Alcorn. The cast was as follows:

Falstaff	Jacob Ming-Trent
Madam Nkechi Ford	Susan Kelechi Watson
Madam Ekua Page	Pascale Armand
Mister Nduka Ford	Gbenga Akinnagbe
Mister Kwame Page	Kyle Scatliffe
Anne Page	Abena
Doctor Caius	David Ryan Smith
Pastor Evans	Phillip James Brannon
Mama Quickly	Shola Adewusi
Shallow	Julian Rozzell Jr.
Fenton/Simple	MaYaa Boateng
Slender/Pistol	Joshua Echebiri
Ensemble	Brandon E. Burton, Branden Lindsay, Ebony Marshall-Oliver, Jarvis D. Matthews, and Jennifer Mogbock

Characters

Note: All characters are Black American and/or of African descent and are to be played by Black actors. Thank you.

Falstaff, *American, the neighborhood trickster.*

Madam Nkechi Ford, *Nigerian, entrepreneur and laundromat owner.*

Madam Ekua Page, *Ghanaian, a socialite.*

Mister Nduka Ford, *Nigerian, very proud and wise.*

Mister Kwame Page, *Ghanaian, well-intentioned and kind.*

Anne Page, *Ghanaian, the beautiful ingenue.*

Doctor Caius, *Senegalese, the flashy neighborhood doctor. To be played by a male-identifying actor.*

Pastor Evans, *Liberian, the loving neighborhood pastor. To be played by a male-identifying actor.*

Mama Quickly, *Nigerian, the fun-loving/scheming "Auntie" of the block.*

Shallow, *Nigerian, the well-intentioned uncle of Slender.*

Fenton, *Ghanaian, honest and pure, also plays Simple, American, errand runner and hustler. To be played by a female-identifying actor.*

Pistol, *American, Falstaff's minion, also plays Slender, Nigerian, nervous but sweet nephew to Shallow.*

Ensemble, *including Nafi, the Hair Braiding Lady and Chiagozie. The role of Chiagozie is gender flexible and may be renamed Chidiadi.*

Setting

116th Street, Harlem, USA.

Time

Present day.

Act One

Scene One

Enter **Shallow**, **Slender**, *and* **Pastor Evans**.

Shallow   Pastor Evans, persuade me not. If he were twenty Falstaffs, he shall not abuse me, Robert Shallow, Esquire.

Pastor Evans   If John Falstaff have committed disparagements unto you, I am of the Church, and will be glad to do my benevolence to make atonements and compromises between you.

Shallow   Hey! My life, o! If I were young again, the sword should end it.

Pastor Evans   It is betta that friends is the sword, and end it. And there is also another device in my brain:

He buzzes.

Page (*within*)   Hello?

Pastor Evans (*into intercom*)   Helllooooo?! God bless your house here.

Page (*within*)   Who is there?

Pastor Evans (*into intercom*)   Here is God's blessing and your friend Pastor Evans and Mister Shallow and here, his nephew young Slender.

Page   Wonderful. I'll be right there.

Pastor Evans (*back to* **Shallow** *and* **Slender**)   There is Anne Page, who is 'de daughter of Mister Kwame Page, which is pretty virginity.

Slender   The beautiful Anne Page? She has brown hair and speaks sweet-sweet like a woman?

Pastor Evans   Eh-heh. It is that very person. If you marry her, then you'll be quite well compensated. She has a very big inheritance. It were a good motion if we leave our pribbles and prabbles, and desire a marriage between Slender and Anne Page.

Slender   I know the young gentlewoman. She has eh, good gifts.

Pastor Evans   Yes, wealth is most certainly a good gift.

Enter **Page**.

Page   I am glad to see your worships well. I thank you for my goat meat, Mister Shallow.

Shallow   Mister Page, I am glad to see you.

Page   And I am glad to see you, good Slender.

Shallow   Is Falstaff here?

Page   He is within, and I would do a good office between you.

Pastor Evans   It is spoke as Christians ought to speak.

Shallow   He hath wronged me, Mister Page, indeed he has. In a word he has!

Enter **Falstaff**.

Page   Here he comes.

Falstaff   Now, Shallow, you complain of me?

Shallow   Where is the money you owe me Falstaff? This shall be answered!

Falstaff   Okay, I will answer it straight: I don't have it. That is now answered.

Shallow *attempts to hit* **Falstaff**, *but everyone holds him back.*

Pastor Evans   Peace! Peace! I pray you.

Enter **Anne Page** *with wine. Like Beyoncé walking onstage, she walks out, maybe in slow motion, wind blows from somewhere, perhaps there's even some entrance music and all of the men marvel at her, namely* **Slender**. *She hits a pose in all her* *magnificent glory and it's clear that* **Slender** *is gob-smacked by her beauty. Her father breaks the spell.*

Slender   O heaven, this is the beautiful Anne Page.

Page   Aye, daughter, carry the palm wine in. We'll drink within.

Anne   Yes, Father.

Anne Page *exits.*

Page   Ah, here are the Merry Wives!

Enter **Madam Ford** *and* **Madam Page** *to some fanfare. They are beautiful, regal socialites of the neighborhood.*

Page   Ekua, bid these gentlemen welcome. How now, Madam Ford?

Falstaff   Madam Ford, by my troth, you are very well met. By your leave, good madam.

He kisses her hand.

Madam Ford (*unimpressed with* **Falstaff**)   Eh-heh.

Page   Come, we have a roast goat meat for dinner. Come, gentlemen, I hope we shall drink down all unkindness.

Shallow *reaches his hand out to* **Falstaff** *for money.* **Page** *stops him.*

Page   Ah-ah! I shall settle this.

Page *pulls some money out.* **Falstaff** *reaches for it, but* **Page** *hands it all to* **Shallow**. *They all go inside except* **Slender**, **Pastor Evans**, *and* **Shallow**. *Enter* **Simple**.

Slender   Eh-eh, Simple?

Simple   Sorry boss.

Slender   Where have you been? You know that I—

Simple (*slight overlap*)   Sorry boss. It's just been a wild day! And then the trains were slow and you know I'm coming from deep in the Bronx!

Slender   Which Bronx? I must wait on myself, must I?

Simple   Sorry, boss!

Shallow (*to* **Slender**—*overlapping*)   Come-come. A word with you, nephew. Here is, as it were, a tender, a kind of tender, made afar off by Pastor Evans here. Are you understanding me?

Slender   Eh-hehn, sir, you shall find me reasonable. If it be so, I shall do that that is reason.

Pastor Evans   Slender. I will describe the matter to you, if you be capacity of it.

Slender   Nay, I will do as my uncle Shallow says.

Pastor Evans   But that is not the question. The question is concerning your marriage.

Shallow   Eh-hehn. There's the point, sir.

Pastor Evans   Marry, is it, the very point of it—to Anne Page.

Slender   Why, if it be so, I will marry her upon any reasonable demands.

Pastor Evans   But can you, eh, affection the woman? Let us command to know that of your mouth, or of your lips, for philosophers say that the lips are the parcel of the mouth.

Shallow   Will you, upon good dowry, marry her?

Slender   I will marry her, sir, at your request. But if there be no great love in the beginning, I hope upon familiarity we will grow more content. But if you say marry her, I will marry her.

Enter **Anne Page**.

Shallow   Here is the beautiful Anne Page.

Anne   Good evening. The dinner is on the table. My father desires your worships' company.

Shallow   I will wait on him, fair Anne.

Pastor Evans   God's blessed will, I will not be absent for grace.

Pastor Evans *and* **Shallow** *go inside.*

Anne (*to* **Slender**)   Will it please your worship to come in, sir?

Slender   No, I thank you, o, heartily; I am very well.

Anne   The dinner attends you, sir.

Slender   I am not hungry, I thank you, o.

Anne   I pray you sir, walk in.

Slender   I had rather walk here, I thank you.

Enter **Page** *and* **Pastor Evans**.

Page   Come, Slender, come. We stay for you.

Slender   Fair Anne, yourself shall go first.

Anne   Not I, sir; pray you, keep on.

Slender   I'll rather be unmannerly than troublesome.

Anne (*unimpressed*)   Eh-heh.

Anne Page *exits inside,* **Slender** *and* **Page** *follow,* **Pastor Evans** *stays.*

Scene Two

Pastor Evans *and* **Simple** *outside on the street.*

Pastor Evans   Simple! Go your ways, and ask of Doctor Caius'. And there dwells one Mama Quickly, which is in the manner of his nurse.

Simple   Okay . . .

Pastor Evans   Give Mama Quickly this letter (*Handing her a paper.*) for she is a woman that knows lovely Anne Page; and the letter is to desire and require her to solicit your boss Slender's desires to Anne Page.

Simple   Awwww . . .

Pastor Evans   I pray you, be gone, o.

Simple *exits.*

Pastor Evans   Now let me finish my dinner; there's plantains and tilapia to come.

Pastor Evans *exits.*

Scene Three

Falstaff's *apartment.* **Pistol** *enters.*

Falstaff   Aye! Pistol!

Pistol   Falstaff! My man!

Falstaff   Let me ask you something—do you know a Ford of this town?

Pistol   Ford?. . . Ford. Yeah, yeah. He is of substance good.

Falstaff   My guy, I will tell you what I am about.

Pistol   Hmph, "what you are about." You are about two yards wide.

Falstaff   No quips now, Pistol. But yes, in the waist, I am about two yards, but I am now about no waste; I am about thrift.

Pistol   Huh?

Falstaff   I want to make love to Ford's wife.

Pistol   Ford's wife?

Falstaff   Yeah man. I spy, a bit of, uh, "entertainment" in her. She discourses; she carves—you know how they like to carve; and she gives the leer of invitation. I can construe the action of her familiar style; and I can hear her saying: "I am yours Falstaff." Now, the report goes, she has all the rule of her husband's purse.

Pistol   Alright. So what's our plan?

Falstaff (*showing two papers*)   I have written a letter to her; and another to Page's wife, who, even now, gave me good eyes too. Sometimes the beam of her view gilded my foot, sometimes my portly belly.

Pistol   Uh huh . . . and the sun shines at night.

Falstaff   Nah man, I'm serious. She did so course over my exteriors with such a greedy intention that the appetite of her eye did seem to scorch me up like a burning glass. She bears the purse too; she is from a region in Ghana, all gold and bounty. I will be cheaters to them both, and they shall be sugar mamas to me; we're gonna have the Ghanaian AND the Nigerian jollof rice! Go bear this letter to Madam Page—and this one to Madam Ford. And then, my friend, I will thrive!. . . I mean . . . We will thrive.

Falstaff *exits.*

Pistol (*aside*)   Y'all heard that? (*Mocks* **Falstaff**.) "I will thrive!" Tuh! Falstaff really thinks I'm stupid. After all these years, he still won't give me what I deserve. But I'm done playing nice. Yeah . . . I will discuss the foolishness of this "love plan" to Ford. I will incense Ford to deal with poison that will possess him with jealousy. Yeah . . . This time, I will finally have my revenge.

He exits.

Scene Four

Doctor Caius*' Clinic. Enter* **Mama Quickly** *and* **Simple***.*

Mama Quickly (*on the phone*)   Ehh! Mister Rugby. Ah, listen here, go to your window and see if you can see my boss, Doctor Caius, coming. Okay. Okay. Bye-bye.

She hangs up, sucks her teeth.

Mama Quickly   Patricia Simple you say your name is?

Simple   Aye yes, for fault of a better one.

Mama Quickly   Eh-heh. And Slender's your boss?

Simple   Yes.

Mama Quickly   Oooo. I should remember him. Does he not hold up his head, as it were, and strut in his gait?

Simple   Yes, indeed, he does.

Mama Quickly   Well, heaven send Anne Page no worse fortune!
Tell Pastor Evans I will do what I can for your boss, Slender. Anne
is a good girl, and I wish—

Phone rings, she picks it up and listens.

Eh-low?

She listens and then hangs up.

Out, alas! Here comes my boss. We shall all be scolded. Run in
here. Go into this closet. He will not stay long.

Simple *goes into the closet. She sings:*

> Hey hey hey, what you say?
> There's nobody in the closet, nay.

She repeats until stopped. Enter **Doctor Caius**.

Doctor Caius   Vat is you sing? I do not like dese toys. Pray you,
go and vetch me in my closet, a box, a green-a box. Do intend vat
I speak? A green-a box.

Mama Quickly   Ay, yes. I'll fetch it for you. (*Aside.*) I am glad
he did not go in himself. If he had found the young woman, he
would have been veeeeeeeeery upset, yeah.

Doctor Caius   Fe, fe, fe, fe! Ma foi, il fait fort chaud. Je m'en
vais a la cour—la grande affaire.

Quickly *and* **Simple** *quietly argue as she tries to get the box for*
Caius. *Eventually they both find it.*

Mama Quickly   Is it this, sir?

Doctor Caius   Oui, mets-le a mon pocket. Depeche, quickly. By
my trot, I tarry too long. Od's me! Qu'ai-j'oublie? Dere is some
simples in my closet dat I vill not for the varld I shall leave behind.

Mama Quickly (*aside*)   Aye! He'll find Simple in there and be
mad!

Doctor Caius (*pulling out* **Simple**)   O diable, diable! Vat is in my closet? Villainy, larron! My rapier!

Mama Quickly   Good boss, be content.

Doctor Caius   Wherefore shall I be content-a?

Mama Quickly   The young woman is honest.

Doctor Caius   So what is de honest woman doing in my closet? Dere is no honest person dat shall come in my closet.

Mama Quickly   I beg you sir, be not so . . . cantankerous. Hear the truth of it. She came on an errand to me from Pastor Evans.

Doctor Caius   Vell?

Simple   Ay, yes. To desire her to—

Mama Quickly   Peace, I pray you.

Doctor Caius   Peace-a your tongue! (*To* **Simple**.) Speak-a your tale.

Simple   To desire this honest gentlewoman, your nurse, to speak a good word to the marvelous Anne Page for my boss in the way of marriage.

Mama Quickly   You see! I'll never put my finger in the fire, and need not to.

Doctor Caius (*to* **Simple**)   Pastor Evans send-a you?—Tarry you a little-awhile.

Doctor Caius *writes.*

Mama Quickly (*aside to* **Simple**)   I am glad he is so quiet . . . For once. But I'll do your boss Slender what good I can. And as for the doctor—look you, for I keep his clinic, and I clean, make the beds, check in, check out, answer phones, paperwork! And do all myself—

Simple (*aside to* **Quickly**)   That is a great charge to come under one body's hand.

Mama Quickly (*aside to* **Simple**)   Are you advised of that? You shall find it a great charge. And to be up early and down late. But notwithstanding—to tell it to you plain—my boss himself is in love with pretty Anne Page. But, I know Anne's mind. That's neither here nor there.

Doctor Caius (*handing paper to* **Simple**)   You, jack'nape, give-a this letter to Pastor Evans. By gar, it is a shallenge. I will cut his throat in de park, and I will teach a scurvy jackanape pastor to meddle or make. I will cut all his two stones. By gar, he shall not have a stone to throw at his dog.

Simple *exits.*

Mama Quickly   Alas, Simple speaks but for her friend.

Doctor Caius   It is no matter-a ver dat. Do not you tell-a me dat I shall have Anne Page for myself? By gar, I vill kill de jack-priest; I will myself to have Anne Page.

Mama Quickly   Trust me, all shall be well. We must give people leave to prate.

Doctor Caius   Visten, if I have not Anne Page, I shall turn your head out of my door.

Mama Quickly   You shall have Anne—

Caius *exits.*

Mama Quickly   Stupid ass. No, I know Anne's mind for that. Never a woman knows more of Anne's mind than I do, nor can do more than I do with her, I thank heaven.

These people. They are going to run up my blood pressure. Let me check it. They stress me too much, o!

Fenton (*within*)   Who's within there?

Mama Quickly   Who's there? O, Fenton! Come-come. I pray you.

Enter **Fenton**.

Fenton   How now, good woman? How are you?

Mama Quickly   The better that it pleases you to ask.

Fenton   So what's the news? How does pretty Anne Page?

Mama Quickly   In truth, and she is pretty, and honest, and gentle, and one that is your friend, I can tell you that by the way, I praise heaven for it.

Fenton   Shall I do anything else? Shall I not lose my suit?

Mama Quickly   In truth, it's all in God's hands. But notwithstanding, Fenton, I'll be sworn on a book that . . . she loves you.

Fenton   Well, I shall see her today. Hold, there's money for thee.

She hands **Mama Quickly** *money.*

Fenton   Let me have thy voice in my behalf. If you see her before me, put in a good word, yeah?

Mama Quickly   In faith, I definitely will.

Fenton   Well, farewell. I am in great haste now.

Mama Quickly   Farewell.

Fenton *exits.*

Truly an honest soul—and Anne loves her! For I know Anne's mind as well as another does.—Out upon it! What have I forgotten?

She exits.

Act Two

Scene One

Madam Page *is getting her hair braided at the hair braiding salon.*

Nafi, the Hair Braiding Lady (*singing along*)

> We give glory to the Lord, He reigns. We give glory to the Lord, He reigns!
> He reigns, He reigns, He reigns. We give glory to the Lord, He reigns!

Madam Page *winces.* **Nafi** *lowers the music.*

Nafi   Too tight?

Madam Page   Yes, a little bit, o.

Nafi, the Hair Braiding Lady (*insincere*)   Sorry, sorry. Your head is just too soft.

Pistol *walks by the shop and then stops when he sees* **Madam Page** *in there. He enters.*

Pistol   Madam Page! I was just in search of you. I have a letter for you. A love letter, most importantly.

Madam Page What? I have escaped love letters in the holiday time of my beauty, and am I now a subject for them?

Pistol *shrugs at* **Madam Page** *and starts to exit, but she stops him.*

Madam Page   Let me see:

Pistol *smiles at the audience as he hands her the letter and then exits. She reads:*

"Ask me no reason why I love you;
You are merry, so am I:
You love palm wine, and so do I:
So let my love be of service to you, Madam Page—
If the love of a soldier can suffice—
    Thine own true love, by day or night,
    Or any kind of light, with all his might,
    For thee to fight,
    Johnny Falstaff."

Wicked, o! Wicked, wicked world! What an unweighed behavior has this drunkard picked—with the devil's name!—out of my con- versation, that he dares in this manner assay me? Why, he hath not been thrice in my company! Hmph!

She winces in pain.

Nafi, the Hair Braiding Lady (*insincere*)   Sorry, sorry.

Phone rings and she answers. Talks incredibly loud.

Eh-low. EH! Salima, how now? . . . Oh, fine-fine. You say what? Oh, let me come. No, no, I'm not busy.

(*To* **Madam Page**.) I'll be right back, yeah?

Nafi *exits. Enter* **Madam Ford**.

Madam Ford   Sista Page! Me, I was just going to come to your house.

Madam Page   Hmmm, trust me, I was coming to you. You don't look well, o.

Madam Ford   Nay, I'll never believe that. And neither should you.

They laugh.

O Sista Page, give me some counsel!

Madam Page   What's going on?

Madam Ford   Here, read, read: perceive. I shall think the worst of fat men as long as I have an eye to make difference of men's liking. I wonder what tempest threw this whale with so many tons of oil in his belly ashore? How shall I be revenged on him? I think the best way is to entertain him with hope till the wicked fire of lust melts him into his own grease. Did you ever hear the like?

Madam Page   Hmph! Word for word! It's only that the name of Page and Ford differs! Here's the twin of thy letter.

Madam Ford (*looks at both letters and is shocked*)   Nooooo!

Madam Page   I bet he has a thousand of these written with mes, o! He will print them, out of doubt; for he cares not what he puts into the press, when he would put us two.

Madam Ford   Why, this is the very same—the very hand, the very words. Who does he think he is fooling?

Madam Page   It makes me almost ready to wrangle with mine own honesty. I'll entertain myself like one that I am not acquainted withal. For, sure, unless he knows some strain in me that I know not myself, he would never have tried to board my "boat of love" in this fury.

Madam Ford   "Boarding" you call it? Chai! I'll be sure to keep him ABOVE deck.

Madam Page   So will I. If he come under my hatches! Aye! I would sink!

Madam Ford   Because he's so big!

They laugh together then settle—all in the same, unison, revengeful octave.

Madam Page   Let's be revenged on him. Let's appoint him a meeting.

Madam Ford   Fine-fine. Tuh—if only my husband saw this letter! It would give eternal food to his jealousy.

They spot **Ford** *and* **Page** *walking outside of the salon.*

Madam Page   Why, look where he comes; and my good man too—he's as far from jealousy as I am from giving him cause, and that, I hope, is an unmeasurable distance.

Madam Ford   You are the happier woman.

Madam Page   Let's consult together against this greasy scoundrel. Come-come.

Madam Ford   Yes! Let's get to the revenge part, o!

They talk aside. Back on the street, **Pistol** *approaches* **Ford** *and* **Page***.*

Pistol   What's up Ford . . . Page.

Ford   Kedu.[1]   **Page**   Eh-yeh.[2]

Pistol   John Falstaff affects thy wife.

They both stop, confused.

Ford   Eh?!

Pistol   John Falstaff affects thy wife.

He woos both high and low, both rich and poor, both young and old, one with another.

Ford   Love my wife?

Pistol   Yup. With liver burning hot. O, odious is the name.

Ford   What name, sir?

Pistol   The horn, I say.

Take heed, have an open eye, for thieves do their work at night. Take heed, because when summer comes, the cuckoo birds do sing. Believe it, Page.

Page (*genuinely confused*)   What?

Pistol (*to* **Page**)   He loves your wife; that's the long and short of it.

Pistol *exits.* **Madam Page** *and* **Madam Ford** *exit the hair braiding salon.*

---

[1]   "Hello" in Igbo.
[2]   "Hello" in Twi.

Madam Page   My Kwame. How are you?

Page (*to* **Madam Page**)   How now, Ekua?

They talk aside.

Madam Ford (*to* **Ford**)   How now, my sweet Nduka? Why are you melancholy?

Ford   I melancholy? I am not melancholy, Nkechi. Weren't you going home?

Madam Ford   Faith, thou hast some crochets in thy head now.— Will you go, Madam Page?

Madam Page   Have with you. You'll come to lunch, Kwame.

Enter **Mama Quickly***.*

Madam Page (*aside to* **Madam Ford**)   Look who's coming. She shall be our messenger to this scoundrel.

Madam Ford   Trust me, I thought of her. She'll fit it, o.

Madam Ford and **Madam Page** (*to* **Quickly**—*overly nice*)   Hiiiiiiii!

Madam Page (*to* **Mama Quickly**)   You have come to see my daughter Anne?

Mama Quickly   Ay, yes. And, I pray, how does she?

Madam Page   Go in with us and see. We have an hour's talk with you.

Madam Page, **Madam Ford**, *and* **Mama Quickly** *go inside.*

Page   How now, Mister Ford?

Ford   You heard what that fool told me, did you not?

Page   Yes, and you heard what he told me?

Ford   Do you think there is truth in it?

Page   If he should intend this voyage toward my wife, I would turn her loose to him, and what he gets more of her than sharp words, let it lie on my head.

Ford   I do not misdoubt my wife, but I would be loath to turn them together. A man may be too confident. I would have nothing lie on my head: I cannot be thus satisfied.

Enter **Shallow**.

Shallow   Good Mister Page, will you go with me? We have a problem in hand. There is a fight to be fought between Pastor Evans the priest, and Doctor Caius.

Ford   Doctor Caius? (*Imitates him.*) "By gar. . . By gar". . . Him?

Shallow   Yes, will you go with me to behold it?

Page   And I have heard the doctor hath good skill with his weapons.

Shallow   Here, men, here. Shall we go?

Page   Have with you. I would rather hear them scold than fight.

Page *and* **Shallow** *exit.*

Ford   Though Page is a secure fool, and stands so firmly on his wife's frailty, I cannot put off my opinion so easily. She was in his company at Page's house, and what they made there I know not.

Well, I will look further into it, and I have a VERY GOOD disguise so Falstaff will not know it is me. If I find her honest I lose not my labor.

But if not, it is labor well bestowed.

He exits.

Scene Two

Back at **Falstaff***'s apartment.* **Mama Quickly** *buzzes.*

Mama Quickly (*offstage/intercom*)   Give your Excellency good morrow.

Falstaff   Good morrow, Mama Quickly.

Falstaff *buzzes her in. Enter* **Mama Quickly**.

Mama Quickly   Shall I have a word or two with you, your Excellency?

Falstaff   You shall have two thousand, fair woman.

Mama Quickly   There is one Madam Ford, sir—I pray, come a little nearer this way.

Falstaff   Well, on; Madam Ford, you say—

Mama Quickly   Why, she's a good creature, yeah. Lord, your Excellency is quite desirable! Well, heaven forgive you and all of us! So, this is the short and the long of it: You have brought her into such a canaries as 'tis wonderful. She has received your letter, for the which she thanks you a thousand times; and she wants you to know that her husband will not be home between eh, ten and eleven.

Falstaff   Ten and eleven. Eh-heh?

Mama Quickly   Eh-heh! Mister Ford, her husband, will be away from home. Alas, the sweet woman leads an ill life with him: He's a very jealous-jealous man, o.

Falstaff   Ten and eleven. Woman, commend me to her; I will not fail her.

Quickly extends her hand for some money, but **Falstaff** *gives her a high five—clearly not what she wanted.*

Mama Quickly   Okay. Good-good. But I have another message for your Excellency. Madam Page has her hearty commendations to you too; and let me tell you in your ear, she's as fartuous a civil modest wife, and one—I tell you—that will not miss you morning nor evening prayer, whoever be the other. And she told me to tell you that her husband seldom leaves the house, but she hopes there will come a time. Surely, I think you have charms, eh! Yes, in truth.

Falstaff   Not I, I assure thee. Setting the attraction of my good parts aside, I have no other charms.

Mama Quickly   Bless your heart!

Falstaff   But I pray thee, tell me this: Has Ford's wife and Page's wife acquainted each other how they love me?

Mama Quickly   That were a jest indeed! They have not so little grace, I hope!

Falstaff   Commend me to them both. There's my money.

He doesn't give her money but does give her a kiss on her hand.

I am in debt to you.

Mama Quickly *exits. Enter* **Pistol**.

Pistol   Falstaff, there's one Mister Brook outside who would like to speak with and be acquainted with you—and has sent you a morning's draft of Jamaican rum.

He hands **Falstaff** *the rum.*

Falstaff   Brook is his name?

Pistol   Yes, Brook.

Falstaff   Call him in. Such brooks are welcome to me, that over-flows such liquor. Ah ha, Madam Ford and Madam Page, have I encompassed you? Cheers!

Pistol *exits.* **Falstaff** *takes a swig of the rum. Enter* **Ford** *dressed as Brook—a man from the islands. He speaks in a Caribbean dialect. This is his "very good" disguise.*

Ford (*as Brook*)   God bless you, brother.

Falstaff   And you, sir. Would you speak with me?

Ford (*as Brook*)   Me make bold ta' press wit' so little preparation upon you.

Falstaff   You're welcome. What's your will?

Ford (*as Brook*)   Mi name's Brook, uh, mon!

Falstaff   Good Mister Brook, I desire more acquaintance of you.

Ford (*as Brook*)   Good Falstaff, I sue for yours—not ta' charge you, for I must let you understand me 'tink me-self in better condition for a lender than you are, the which has something emboldened me ta' this unseasoned intrusion; for they say if money go before, all ways do lie open.

Falstaff   Money talks. Always has, always will.

Ford (*as Brook*)   Truth, and I have a bag of money 'ere that troubles me.

He sets it down.

If you will help ta' bear it, Falstaff, take all, or half, for easing me of the carriage.

Falstaff   Fam, I know not how I may deserve to be your porter.

Ford (*as Brook*)   I will tell you, brother, if you will give me the hearing.

Falstaff   Speak, good Mister Brook. I shall be glad to be your servant.

Ford (*as Brook*)   There is a gentlewoman in this town, her husband's name's Ford. I have long loved her and, I protest to you, bestowed much on her, followed her with a doting observance, engrossed opportunities to meet her, bought many presents to give to her. Briefly, I have pursued her as love has pursued me— which is, you know, like all the time.

Anyway, whatsoever I have merited, either in my mind or in my means, I have yet to receive any reward for all the good I've done.

Falstaff   Have you received no promise of satisfaction at her hands?

Ford (*as Brook*)   Neva.

Falstaff   Have you importuned her to such a purpose?

Ford (*as Brook*)   Neva.

Falstaff   Of what quality was your love, then?

Ford (*as Brook*)   Like a fair house built on another man's ground, so that I have lost me edifice by mistaking the place where I built it.

Falstaff   To what purpose have you unfolded this to me?

Ford (*as Brook*)   When I have told you that, I have told you all. Some say that though she appears honest, in other places, her behavior is suggestive of something more suspicious. Now, Falstaff, here is the heart of my purpose: You are a gentleman of excellent breeding, admirable discourse, and of great admittance.

Falstaff (*flattered*)   Oh, come on man!

Ford (*as Brook*)   Believe it, for you know it! 'Dere is the money.

He points to the bag.

Spend it, spend it, spend more, spend all me have; only give me so much of your time in exchange of it as to lay an amiable siege to the honesty of this woman. Use your art of wooing, win her to consent to you.

Falstaff (*taking the bag*)   Mister Brook, I will first make bold with your money. Next, give me your hand. And last, as I am a gentleman, you shall, if you will, enjoy Ford's wife.

Ford (*as Brook*)   Ayyyyye! Good good Good. Very good.

Falstaff   I say you shall.

Ford (*as Brook*)   Want no money, Mister Falstaff, you shall want none.

Falstaff   Want no Madam Ford, Mister Brook; you shall want none. But ummm-I'mma be with her.

Ford (*as Brook*)   Huh?

Falstaff   Yeah, yeah, I may tell you, by her own appointment. Between ten and eleven, for at that time the jealous, rascally fool, her husband, will be gone. If you come to me at night: You shall know how I speed.

Ford (*as Brook*)   I am blessed in your acquaintance. And uh . . . ya' know who Ford is?

Falstaff   That fool! No. I know him not. But they say the jealous wittolly knave has masses of money, for which his wife seems to me well-favored. I will use her as the key of the cuckoldy rogue's coffer.

Ford (*as Brook*)   I would you knew Ford, sir, that ya' might avoid him if you saw him.

Falstaff   Please, I ain't worried about him! I will stare him out of his wits, I will awe him with my club; I shall hang like LeBron James over the cuckold's horns. And this, Mister Brook, you shalt know him for knave and cuckold. Come to me soon at night.

Falstaff *exits.*

Ford (*aside*)   Who says this is improvident jealousy? My wife has sent to him, the hour is set, the match is made. Would any man have thought this? Now you see the hell of having a false woman?! My bed shall be abused, my coffers ransacked, my reputation done. "Cuckold," "Cuckold, oooo!" The devil himself has not such a name. Page is an ass, a foolish ass. He will trust his wife. (*Sucks teeth.*) He will not be jealous. Ha! God be praised for my jealousy! Eleven o'clock the hour. I will prevent this, detect my wife, be revenged on Falstaff, and laugh at Page. Better three hours too soon than a minute too late. Cuckold, cuckold, cuckold! Me? No, no, no!

He exits.

Act Three

Enter **Pastor Evans** *with a book and a baseball bat.* **Simple** *meets him on the street.*

Pastor Evans I pray you now, good Slender's servingman and friend Simple by your name, which way have you looked for Doctor Caius, that calls himself a physician?

Simple Marry, sir, the Petty-ward, the Park-ward, every way but the town way.

Pastor Evans I most vehemently desire you will also look that way.

Simple I will, sir.

Simple *holds out her hand for some money.* **Pastor** *gives her some before she runs off and exits.*

Pastor Evans Bless my soul, how sick I am and trembling of mind! I shall be glad if he has deceived me. How scared I am! Why does Doctor Caius want to fight me? Why would he do this? Oh Lord please, bless my soul!

He sings:

> Amazing grace, where are You now?
> I need You here with meeee.
> I've said a prayer, what? Can't You hear,
> Lord, please show up for me.

Mercy on me, I am very much about to cry.

Enter **Simple**.

Simple   Hey, look out here! He is coming this way, Pastor Evans!

Pastor Evans   He's welcome. Heaven prosper the right!

Pastor Evans *tries to be brave but then runs and hides. Enter* **Caius**, **Page**, **Shallow**, *and* **Slender**.

Doctor Caius   By gar, he is de coward jack-priest of de vorld. I pray you bear witness. He is no come.

Shallow   He is the wiser man, Doctor Caius. He is a curer of souls, and you a curer of bodies. If you should fight, you go against the hair of your professions. Is it not true, Mister Page?

Page   Mister Shallow, you have yourself been a great fighter, though now a man of peace.

Shallow   Eh, by God's body, Mister Page! Though I now be old and of the peace, if I see a sword out, my finger itches to make one. Though we are justices and doctors and churchmen, Mister Page, we have some salt of our youth in us. We are the sons of women, Mister Page.

Anne Page *comes out of her house and sweeps her stoop.*

Slender (*aside*)   Ah, sweet Anne Page!

Simple *scares* **Pastor Evans** *and he drops his baseball bat.*

Pastor Evans   Sweet baby Jesus!

Page *sees* **Pastor Evans**.

Page   Good Pastor Evans, put away your weapon.

Shallow   So do you, good Doctor Caius.

Doctor Caius   By gar, you are de coward, de jack-dog, de rat!

Pastor Evans and **Doctor Caius**   Don't hold me back! Don't hold me back!

Pastor Evans   Jesus, take the wheel!

They begin "fighting," but it's not much of a fight.

Pastor Evans (*aside to* **Caius**)   Pray you, let us not be laughingstocks to other men's humors.

Doctor Caius   You are ze laughingstock!

They separate.

Pastor Evans   I will prescribe a beating to you, Doctor!

Doctor Caius   Diable!

They fight again.

Pastor Evans (*aside to* **Caius**)   I desire you in friendship!

Doctor Caius (*aside to* **Pastor Evans**)   Vy did you send-a that letter?

Pastor Evans (*aside to* **Caius**)   I just want love to win!

They continue to fight.

(*Overlapping.*) Rogue!

Doctor Caius (*overlapping*)   Villainy!

Pastor Evans (*overlapping*)   Crook!

Doctor Caius (*overlapping*)   Grossier!

Pastor Evans (*overlapping*)   Bad doctor!

Doctor Caius (*overlapping*)   Idiot![3]

Page *stops the fight.*

Page   Peace, I say! Hear me. Am I a schemer? Am I subtle? Shall I lose my doctor? No! He gives me the potions and the motions. Shall I lose my pastor, my priest? No, he gives me the proverbs and the no-verbs. (*To* **Caius**.) Give me your hand, so. (*To* **Pastor Evans**.) Give me your hand, so. Your hearts are mighty, your skins are whole, and let spilled wine be the issue.

Pastor Evans *and* **Doctor Caius** *consider this and then relent.*

Pastor Evans (*extends his hand—olive branch*)   Peace?

[3]   "ee-Djoh!"

Doctor Caius (*shakes his hand back*)   Pay-ce.

Pastor Evans *and* **Caius** *make up. All is well. They all cheer with relief.*

Page   Follow me, brothers of peace. Follow, follow, follow.

They all exit happily and singing together, but **Slender** *lags behind, still staring at* **Anne***.*

Slender (*aside*)   Eh! That Anne Page, o! She is so fine-fine. What is she doing to my heart?!

All   Follow!

Slender   Oh! Sorry.

Slender *exits.*

Scene Two

Enter **Ford** *and* **Madam Page***.*

Ford   Well met, Madam Page. Where are you going?

Madam Page   To see your wife. Is she in?

Ford   As idle as she may hang together, for want of company. You two—I think if your husbands were dead, you would marry.

Madam Page   Be sure of that—two other husbands, ha! Your wife is there indeed?

Ford   Indeed, she is.

Madam Page   By your leave, sir. I am sick till I see her.

Madam Page *exits.*

Ford   Has Page any brains? Any eyes? Does he think? Good plots they are laid, and our revolted wives share damnation together. Well, I will show him, pluck the borrowed veil of modesty from the so-seeming Madam Page, divulge Page himself for a secure and willful cuckold, and to these violent proceedings all my neighbors shall cry aim.

A clock strikes.

The clock gives me my cue, and my assurance bids me search:
There I shall find Falstaff. Let me see.

Enter **Page**, **Shallow**, **Evans**, **Caius**, *and* **Slender**.

Page   Well met, Mister Ford.

Ford   I have good cheer, and I pray you all go with me.

Shallow   I must excuse myself, Mister Ford.

Slender   And so must I, sir. I have an appointment to dine with
the dazzling Anne Page, and I would not break with her for more
money than I'll speak of.

Shallow   We have lingered about a match between Anne
Page and my nephew Slender, and this day we shall have our
answer.

Slender   I hope I have your good will, Father Page.

Shallow *and* **Slender** *exit.*

Page   You have, Slender. I stand wholly for you.—But my wife,
Doctor Caius, is for you altogether.

Doctor Caius   Ay, by gar, and your daughter is in love-a with me!
My nursh-a Quickly tell me so mush.

Ford   I ask you heartily, some of you go with me. Besides your
cheer, you shall have sport. I will show you a monster. Doctor
Caius, you shall go; so shall you, Pastor Evans, and you, Mister
Page. I will show you a monster.

They all exit.

Scene Three

Madam Ford *and* **Madam Page** *are at the Ford Laundromat.*

Madam Ford   Hey! Chiagozie?! (*Barely waits for a response,
then louder.*) CHIAGOZIE!

Madam Page   Quickly, quickly! Is the laundry basket—

Madam Ford   I warrant. What, Chiagozie, I say!

Enter **Chiagozie** *with a large laundry basket.*

Madam Page   Come, come, come.

Madam Ford   Here, set it down.

Madam Page   Give her the charge. We must be brief.

Madam Ford   Marry, as I told you before, Chiagozie, be ready here, hard by, in the back, and, when I suddenly call you, come forth. And without any pause or staggering, take this basket. That done, trudge with it in all haste, and empty it in the muddy ditch close by the river.

Madam Page   You will do it?

Madam Ford   I have told her over and over. Go, and come when you are called.

Chiagozie *exits.*

Madam Ford   Sista Page, remember your cue, eh.

Madam Page   I'll remember, but if I do not act it, hiss me.

Madam Ford   Go to, then.

Madam Page *exits. Enter* **Falstaff**. *Perhaps he sings this. Or gives his best Barry White spoken word version. Suffice it to say, this is a performance for* **Falstaff**.

Falstaff   "Have I caught thee, my heavenly jewel?" Why, now let me die, for I have lived long enough. This is the period of my ambition. O, this blessed hour! I love you baby!

Madam Ford   O, sweet Falstaff!

Falstaff   Madam Ford, I cannot cog. I cannot prate, Madam Ford: Now shall I sin in my wish: I would your husband were dead. I would make thee my woman.

Madam Ford   Me? Your woman? Aye, Johnny? Alas, I should be a pitiful lady.

Falstaff   What made me love thee? Let that persuade thee there's something extraordinary in thee. Come, I cannot duplicitously say—

Madam Ford   Duplicitici-what?

Falstaff   —that thou art this or thou are that. But I love you, no one but you; and you deserve it.

Madam Ford   Well, heaven knows how I love you, and you shall one day find it.

Falstaff   Oooh. . . Keep in that mind. Cause I'mma deserve it!

Madam Ford   Nay, I must tell you, so you do, or else I could not be in that mind . . .

Madam Page *knocks at the door.*

Ah! Here's Madam Page at the door.

Falstaff   She shall not see me. I will hide myself.

Madam Ford   Pray you, do so. She's a very tattling woman.

Falstaff *hides. Enter* **Madam Page**. *Now it's time for the wives to perform.*

Madam Ford   What's the matter? How now?

Madam Page   O Sista Ford, what have you done? You're shamed, you're overthrown, you're undone forever!

Madam Ford   What's the matter, Ekua?

Madam Page   O well-a-day, Nkechi, having an honest man to your husband, to give him such cause of suspicion!

Madam Ford   What cause of suspicion?

Madam Page   You say what? How am I mistook in you!

Madam Ford   Why, alas, what's the matter?

Madam Page   Your husband's coming here, woman, to search for a gentleman that he says is here now, by your consent, to take an ill advantage of his absence. You are undone.

Madam Ford   'Tis not so, I hope.

Madam Page   Pray heaven it be not so, that you have such a man here! But 'tis most certain your husband's coming to search for such a one. I come before to tell you. If you know yourself clear, why, I am glad of it; but if you have a friend here, convey, convey him out. Be not amazed, call all your senses to you, defend your reputation, or bid farewell to your good life forever.

Madam Ford   What shall I do? There is a gentleman, my dear friend; and I fear not mine own shame so much as his peril.

Madam Page   Shame on you, o! Your husband's here at hand: O, how have you deceived me!—Look, here is a basket: If he is of any reasonable stature, he may creep in here, and throw foul linen upon him, as if it were going to washing;. . . It's bleaching time! (*Smiles.*)

Madam Ford   He's too big to go in there. What shall I do?

Falstaff *runs out.*

Falstaff   Let me see it! Let me see it! Let. Me. See. It!

Madam Page   What, Falstaff?

Falstaff (*caught*)   Heeeyyyyy Madam Page! (*Back to the matter at hand—the laundry basket.*) I'll in, I'll in. Follow your friend's counsel. I'll in.

Madam Page (*aside to him*)   Are these your letters?

Falstaff (*aside to* **Madam Page**)   Ummm, well . . . you know I love thee and none but thee.—

Madam Page *rolls her eyes and starts to help place* **Falstaff**, *who climbs into the laundry basket; they cover him with dirty clothes.*

Madam Page   Call Chiagozie, Sista Ford.— (*To* **Falstaff**.) You dissembling foolish man!

Madam Ford   Chiagozie! Chiagozie!

Enter **Chiagozie**.

Madam Ford   Go, take up these clothes here quickly. Quickly! Come.

Enter **Ford***,* **Page***,* **Evans***, and* **Caius***.*

Ford   Pray you, come near. If I suspect without cause, why then make sport at me, then let me be your jest, I deserve it.—How now? Whither bear you this?

Madam Ford (*sarcasm*)   Why, what have you to do whither she bear it? You were best meddle with laundry washing!

Chiagozie *exits with the laundry basket, more like struggles with it.*

Ford (*to the men*)   Anyway, gentlemen, I have dreamed tonight; I'll tell you my dream. Here, here, here be my keys. Ascend my chambers. Search, seek, find out. I'll warrant we'll unkennel the fox. Let me stop this way first.

He locks the door.

So now, escape, you adulterer!

Page   Good Mister Ford, be contented; you wrong yourself too much.

Ford   True, Mister Page. Up, gentlemen. You shall see sport now—now. Follow me, gentlemen.

He goes to the back of the laundromat in search of **Falstaff***.*

Pastor Evans   This is very fantastical humor and jealousy.

Page   Let's follow him, gentlemen; see the issue of his search.

Page*,* **Pastor Evans***, and* **Caius** *follow* **Ford***. Once they are gone,* **Madam Page** *and* **Madam Ford** *try to muffle their laughter/ excitement.*

Madam Page   Is there not a double excellency in this?

Madam Ford   I don't know which pleases me better—that my husband is deceived, or Falstaff.

Madam Page   What a taking was he in, when your husband asked about the basket!

Madam Ford   I think my husband hath some special suspicion of Falstaff's being here, for I never saw him so gross in his jealousy till now.

Madam Page   I will lay a plot to try that, and we will yet have more tricks with Falstaff. His dissolute disease will scarce obey this medicine.

Madam Ford   Shall we send that crazy Mama Quickly to him, and excuse his throwing into the water, and give him another hope, to betray him to another punishment?

Madam Page   We will do it: Let him be sent for tomorrow around eight o'clock to have amends.

Enter **Ford**, **Page**, **Doctor Caius**, *and* **Pastor Evans**.

Ford   I cannot find him. Maybe the scoundrel bragged of that he could not compass.

Madam Page (*aside to* **Madam Ford**)   Did you hear that?

Madam Ford   You use me well, darling, do you?

Ford   Eh-heh, I do so.

Madam Ford   Heaven make you better than your thoughts!

Ford   Amen!

Madam Page   You do yourself mighty wrong, Mister Ford.

Ford   Yes, yes. I must bear it.

Pastor Evans   If there be anybody here, heaven forgive my sins on the day of judgment!

Doctor Caius   By gar, nor I too; there is nobodies.

Page   Look here, Mister Ford, are you not ashamed? What spirit, what devil suggests this imagination?

Ford   This is my fault, Mister Page. I suffer for it.

Pastor Evans   You suffer for a bad conscience. Your wife is as honest a woman as I will desire among five thousand, and five hundred too.

Doctor Caius   By gar, I see this as an honest woman.

Ford   Come, come, I pray you pardon me; I will hereafter make known to you why I have done this. Come walk in the park. Come, wife, come, Madam Page.

Madam Page *and* **Madam Ford** *suck their teeth at him and exit.*

Page (*to* **Ford***,* **Caius***, and* **Pastor Evans**)   I do invite you tomorrow morning to my house for breakfast; after, we'll go to the park for some bird-watching together. Shall it be so?

Ford   Anything.

Pastor Evans   If there is one, I shall make two in the company.

Doctor Caius   If there be one or two, I shall make-a the turd.

Ford   Pray you go, gentlemen.

They all exit.

Scene Four

Enter **Fenton** *and* **Anne Page***.*

Fenton   I see I cannot get your father's love; Therefore no more send me to him, sweet Anne.

Anne   Alas, how then?

Fenton *takes* **Anne***'s hand and kisses it.*

Fenton   Why, thou must be thyself.

Your father doth object

And tells me 'tis a thing impossible

I should love thee.

Anne   Oh . . . so you think he tells you true?

Fenton   No, God so speed me in my time to come.

Anne   Then seek my father's love. Seek it now.

They talk aside. Enter **Shallow**, **Slender**, *and* **Mama Quickly**.

Shallow   Break their talk, Mama Quickly. My nephew shall speak for himself.

Mama Quickly (*to* **Anne**)   Excuse me, Slender would speak a word with you.

Anne   I'll come to him.

Mama Quickly   And how does good Fenton?

Pray you, a word with you.

Fenton *and* **Quickly** *talk aside.*

Anne (*aside*)   This, Slender, is my father's choice. He is perfectly nice and is as handsome as his worth.

And while I vow to always do the right thing and make my father proud

It is Fenton who has my heart today, tomorrow, and forever.

She walks closer to **Slender**.

Shallow (*to* **Slender**)   She's coming; to her, nephew! O boy, tell her about your father!

Slender   I had a father, exquisite Anne. Yeah, yeah. He was so funny. My uncle can tell you good jests of him. Pray you, good uncle, tell Anne Page the jest how my father stole all this toilet paper from the store.

Shallow   Beautiful Anne, my nephew loves you.

Slender   Yes, that I do, as well as I love any woman.

Shallow   He will maintain you like a gentlewoman.

Anne   Good Mister Shallow, let him woo for himself.

Shallow   Marry, I thank you for it. I thank you for that good comfort.—She calls you, nephew. I'll leave you.

He steps aside.

Anne   Now, Slender . . .

Slender   Now, good Anne Page . . .

Anne   What is your will?

Slender   My will? God's heartlings, that's a pretty jest indeed! I haven't made my will yet, I thank heaven: I am not such a sickly creature, praise God. Hallelujah!

Anne   No, Slender, I mean what do you want from me?

Slender (*nervous beyond words*)   Truly, for mine own part, I would want little or nothing from you, except your heart of course.

Your father and my uncle have made motions on my behalf.

If it be my luck, that's fine-fine; if not, may fate reward the lucky man. They can tell you how things go better than I can. You can ask your father.

Enter **Page** *and* **Madam Page**.

Slender   Oh look, here he comes! (*Quietly to* **Page**.) Help me!

Page   Now, Slender—love him, daughter Anne—

He sees **Fenton** *and becomes upset.*

Page   Why, how now? Why is Fenton here?

(*To* **Fenton**.) You wrong me, thus still to haunt my house. I told you, my daughter is disposed of.

Fenton   Please, Mister Page, be not impatient.

Madam Page   Good Fenton, come not to my child.

Page   She is no match for you.

Fenton   Sir, will you hear me?

Page   No, good Fenton.—

Come, Mister Shallow; come, son Slender, in.—

Knowing my mind, you wrong me, Fenton.

Page, **Shallow**, *and* **Slender** *go inside.*

Mama Quickly (*aside to* **Fenton**)   Speak to Madam Page.

Fenton   Good Madam Page, for that I love your daughter

In such a righteous fashion as I do,

Perforce, against all checks, rebukes, and manners,

I must advance the colors of my love

And not retire. Let me have your good will.

Anne   Good mother, do not marry me to that fool.

Madam Page   Don't worry; I seek you a better husband.

Mama Quickly (*aside*)   That's my boss, Doctor Caius.

Anne   Please! I'd rather be set quick in the earth

And beaten to death with a bag of cocoyams!

Madam Page   Come, trouble not yourself. Good Fenton,

I will not be your friend, nor enemy.

My daughter I will question how she loves you, and as I find her, so am I affected. Till then, farewell; she must go inside,

Her father will be angry.

Fenton   Farewell, gentle Madam. Farewell, dearest Anne.

Madam Page *goes inside.* **Anne** *sneaks and blows* **Fenton** *a kiss before she follows inside to her mother.*

Mama Quickly   Well, look at that: This is my doing now! I told her, I said, "Madam Page—would you set your child up with a fool or a physician? No! Look on Fenton!" Yes, this is my doing, now.

Fenton   I thank you; and I pray, at some point tonight,

Give my sweet Anne this ring.—There's for thy pains.

She gives her money and a ring.

Mama Quickly   Now heaven send you good fortune.

Fenton *exits.*

Mama Quickly   A kind heart she hath. One would run through fire and water for such a kind heart. But yet I would my boss had Anne Page, or I would Slender had her; or, in sooth, I would Fenton had her. I will do what I can for all three of them, for so I have promised and I'll be as good as my word.

Well, I must of another errand to Falstaff from the two madams. What a beast am I to slack it!

She exits.

Scene Five

Enter **Falstaff**. *He is soaking wet after being thrown into the river/ sewer.*

Falstaff   Have I lived to be carried in a basket like a box of rotten meat and to be thrown in the river? You may know by my size that I have a kind of alacrity in sinking: If the bottom were as deep as hell, I should drown—a death that I abhor; for the water swells a man; and what a thing should I have been when I had been swelled! I should have been a mountain of mummy.

Enter **Mama Quickly**.

Mama Quickly   By your leave, I cry you mercy. Give your worship good morrow. I come to you from Madam Ford.

Falstaff   Madam Ford? I have had enough of ford. I was thrown into the ford, I have my belly full of ford.

Mama Quickly   Alas the day, good heart, that was not her fault.

She does so take on with her men: They mistook their erection, pardon, direction.

Falstaff   So did I mine, to build upon a foolish woman's promise.

Mama Quickly   Well, she laments, sir, for it, that it would yearn your heart to see it. Her husband goes this morning birding. She desires you once more to come to her, between eight and nine. I must carry her word quickly; she'll make amends with you, I promise you.

Falstaff   Well, I will visit her; tell her so, and tell her to think what a man is. Let her consider his frailty, and then judge of my merit.

Mama Quickly   I will tell her.

Falstaff   Do so. Between nine and ten, you say?

Mama Quickly   Eight and nine, sir.

Falstaff   Well, be gone. I will not miss her.

Mama Quickly   Peace be with you, sir.

Mama Quickly *exits.*

Falstaff   I marvel I hear not of Mister Brook; he sent me word to stay within. I like his money well.

Intercom buzz.

Ford (*as Brook—over the intercom*)   God bless you, mon'.

Falstaff   Oh, here he comes.

Door buzz. Enter **Ford** *disguised as Brook.*

Falstaff   Now, Mister Brook, you come to know what hath passed between me and Ford's wife.

Ford (*as Brook*)   That indeed, Falstaff, is my business.

Falstaff   Mister Brook, I will not lie to you. I was at her house the hour she appointed me.

Ford (*as Brook*)   And how did it go?

Falstaff   Very ill-favoredly, Mister Brook.

Ford (*as Brook*)   How so, sir? Did she change her mind?

Falstaff   Nah, but her husband dwelling in a continual state of jealousy, comes to me in the instant of our encounter, after we had embraced, kissed, protested, and, as it were, spoke the prologue of our comedy; and, at his heels, a rabble of his companions that were provoked and instigated by his distemper, and, therefore followed him to search for his wife's lover, aka me!

Ford (*as Brook*)   What, while you were there?

Falstaff   While I was there, fam!

Ford (*as Brook*)   And did he search for you, and could not find you?

Falstaff   Can I finish? Okay, so as good luck would have it, Madam Page comes in, gives intelligence of Ford's approach, and in her invention, and Ford's wife's distraction, they conveyed me into a laundry basket.

Ford (*as Brook*)   A laundry basket?!

Falstaff   A laundry basket! Rammed me in with foul shirts and smocks, socks, foul stockings, greasy napkins, that, man, when I tell you-that was the rankest compound of villainous smell that ever offended a nostril.

Ford (*as Brook*)   And how long were you in there?

Falstaff   Let me tell you Mister Brook cause WHEW! What I have suffered to bring this woman to evil for your good. I was crammed in the basket and then one of Ford's knaves, his hinds, was called forth by his wife to carry me, and met the jealous knave at the door, who asked her once or twice what was in the basket. I quaked for fear lest the lunatic fool would have searched it, but fate protected me! On went he for a search, and away went I in foul clothes, half stewed in grease. It was a miracle to escape suffocation! Think of that, Mister Brook. Think about it Mister Brook! Think about it Mister Brook—Think. Of. That. Ugh! It was so stinky.

Ford (*as Brook*)   In good sadness, sir, me sorry that for my sake you have suffered all this. My suit, then, is desperate: You'll undertake her no more?

Falstaff   Well . . . Her husband is this morning gone bird-watching. I have received from her another embassy of meeting. Between eight and nine is the hour.

Ford (*as Brook*)   But it's past eight already, sir.

Falstaff   Is it? I will then address me to my appointment. Come to me at your convenient leisure, and you shall know how I speed; and the conclusion shall be crowned with your enjoying her. See you soon, fam. You shall have her, Mister Brook. Mister Brook, you shall cuckold Ford.

Falstaff *exits.*

Ford   Hey God! Is this a vision? Is this a dream? Do I sleep? Mister Ford, awake! Awake, Mister Ford! This 'tis to be married, this 'tis to have linen and foul laundry baskets! Well, I will now take the lecher. He cannot escape me.—It is impossible he should. But, lest the devil that guides him should aid him, I will search impossible places. Though what I am I cannot avoid, yet to be what I would not shall not make me tame. If I have horns to make one mad, let the proverb go with me: I shall be horn-mad, o!

He exits.

Act Four

Scene One

Madam Ford *is at the laundromat. She sits behind the desk, folding clothes, doing work, etc. She keeps staring at her watch and looking out of the window in anticipation. As she paces, she starts to hum to herself. She sings the chorus of "Johnny" by Yemi Alade and gets carried away. If you cannot/do not want to procure the rights to this song, please use alternative verse provided below. It should feel like a fun Afrobeats song.*

Madam Ford (*alternative verse. Sings.*)

Oh Johnny Johnny . . .
You're late boo boo
Oh Johnny Johnny
Do you want fufu?

She starts getting carried away.

Oh Johnny Johnny
I'm looking for you.
Oh Johnny Johnny
I'm coming for you!

Falstaff *enters. He enjoys watching* **Madam Ford** *dance and sing.* **Falstaff** *clears his throat and* **Madam Ford** *gets startled.*

Madam Ford   Eh, Johnny . . . Johnny Falstaff!

Falstaff   Madam Ford, your sorrow has eaten up my suffering. I see you are obsequious in your love, and I profess requital to a hair's breadth, not only, Madam Ford, in the simple office of love, but in all the accoutrement, compliment, and ceremony of it. But are you sure of your husband now?

Madam Ford   He's bird-watching, sweet Johnny.

They start to dance/flirt/etc. And just as **Falstaff** *thinks things about to get spicy,* **Madam Page** *knocks on the door.*

Madam Page (*within*)   Hello! Sista Ford! Hello!

Madam Ford   Man! She is always wrecking my flow!

Madam Ford   Step into the back, Johnny.

Falstaff *exits. Enter* **Madam Page***.*

Madam Page   How now, Nkechi, who's here besides yourself?

Madam Ford   Why, none but mine own staff.

Madam Page   Indeed?

Madam Ford   No, certainly. (*Whispers.*) Speak louder.

Madam Page   Truly, I am so glad you have nobody here.

Madam Ford   Why?

Madam Page   What do you mean, "why" woman? Your husband is in his old tricks again. He so takes on yonder with my husband, so rails against all married mankind, so curses all Eve's daughters, and so buffets himself on the forehead, crying "Look out, o! Look out!" I am glad that that eiiii obolo[4] is not here.

Madam Ford   Why, does he talk of him?

Madam Page   Of none but him, and swears he was carried out, the last time he searched for him, in a basket; protests to my husband he is now here, and has drawn him and the rest of their company from their sport, to make another experiment of his suspicion. But I am glad that Falstaff is not here. Now he shall see his own foolery.

Madam Ford   How near is he, Sista Page?

Madam Page   Hard by, at street end. He will be here soon.

---

[4]   "eee-oh-bowl-oh"—it means "large person" in Twi.

Madam Ford Dear God! I am undone. He is here!

Madam Page Why, then you are utterly shamed, and he's but a dead man. Away with him, away with him: better shame than murder.

Madam Ford Which way should he go? How should I bestow him? Shall I put him into the basket again?

Enter **Falstaff**.

Falstaff Nooooooo! I'll come no more in the laundry basket! May I not go out before he comes?

Madam Page Alas, three of Mister Ford's brothers watch the door with weapons, that none shall issue out.

Falstaff What shall I do? I'll creep onto the fire escape.

Madam Ford He will seek there on my word.

Madam Page Creep into the storage closet.

Falstaff Where is it?

Madam Ford Eh-eh! There is no hiding you here.

Madam Page And, if you go out in your own semblance, you die, Johnny—unless you go out disguised.

Madam Ford How might we disguise him?

Madam Page Me, I don't know. There is no garment big enough for him.

Falstaff Good hearts, devise something! Anything!

Madam Ford My auntie's uncle's cousin . . . the old man of Benin, has some clothes in the back.

Madam Page On my word, it will serve him. He's as big as Falstaff is. And there's his big dashiki and matching walking cane too. Run in and hide, Johnny.

Madam Ford Go, go, sweet Johnny. Madam Page and I will look for those things for you.

Madam Page   Quick, quick! We'll come dress you straight away.

Falstaff *exits.*

Madam Ford   I would my husband would meet him in
this shape! He cannot stand the old man of Benin; he swears
he's a soothsayer or witch doctor something-something and
has forbade him from coming here. He has even threatened
to beat him.

Madam Page   Heaven guide him to thy husband's cudgel, and
the devil guide his cudgel afterwards!

Madam Ford   But is my husband coming?

Madam Page   Eh, in good sadness is he, and talks of the basket
too, howsoever he has had intelligence.

Madam Ford   Eh-heh. I'll bring the basket straight.

Madam Page   Dishonest goat! We cannot misuse him enough.

Madam Ford *exits.*

Madam Page   We'll leave proof, by that which we will do,

Wives may be merry and yet honest too.

Enter **Madam Ford** *with* **Chiagozie** *and a stuffed laundry basket.
The shape of it looks similar to how* **Falstaff** *'s was when he
escaped.*

Madam Ford   Go, take the basket again. Your boss is hard at the
door. If he bid you to set it down, obey him. Quickly, dispatch.
Come-come.

Chiagozie *is not happy about this.* **Madam Page** *and* **Madam
Ford** *exit to the back of the laundromat. Enter* **Ford**, **Page**,
Shallow, **Caius**, *and* **Evans**.

Ford   Ay, but if it prove true, Mister Page, have you any way
then to unfool me again?—

He sees **Chiagozie** *with the basket and stops her.*

Ford   Set down the basket, villain!

Chiagozie *places the basket in the center of the room.*

Ford   Somebody call my wife. O, you panderly rascals, there's a knot, a gang, a pack, a conspiracy against me. Now shall the devil be shamed.—What, wife, I say! Come, come forth: Behold what honest clothes you send forth to bleaching!

Page   Why, this passes, Mister Ford! You are not to go loose any longer, you must be caught.

Shallow   Indeed, Mister Ford, this is not well indeed.

Ford   So say I too, sir.

Enter **Madam Ford**.

Ford   Come here, Madam Ford.— Madam Ford, the honest woman, the modest wife, the virtuous creature that has the jealous fool to her husband! I suspect without cause, do I?

Madam Ford   Heaven be my witness you do, if you suspect me of any dishonesty.

Ford   Well said, brazen-face, hold it out!—Come here, girl.

Chiagozie *stands behind the basket.*

Madam Ford   Are you not ashamed? Let the clothes alone.

Chiagozie *retreats away from the basket, confused about what to do.*

Ford   As I am a man, there was one conveyed out of here yesterday in this basket. Why wouldn't he be there again? I am sure he is. My intelligence is true, my jealousy is reasonable.

Madam Ford   If you find a man there, he shall die a flea's death.

Ford   A-Ha!

Ford *empties the basket. Feels a little dumb.*

Here's no man.

Doctor Caius   No man . . .

Shallow   This is not well, Mister Ford, this wrongs you.

Pastor Evans   Mister Ford, you must pray, and not follow the imaginations of your own heart: This is jealousies.

Doctor Caius   Jealousies . . .

Ford   Well, he's not here I seek for.

Page   No, nor nowhere else but in your brain.

Doctor Caius   Your brain . . .

Ford   Help to search this one time. If I find not what I seek, show no color for my extremity, let me forever be your table-sport. Satisfy me once more, once more search with me.

Chiagozie *refills the basket and carries it off.*

Madam Ford (*calling offstage*)   Sista Page! Come you and the old man out. My husband will come into the back.

Ford   "Old man"? What old man is that?

Madam Ford   Why, it is my auntie's uncle's cousin. The old man of Benin.

Ford   The witch doctor?! Have I not forbid him and his family from here? My property? My place of business?! Come out, you witch, you! Come out, I say!

He grabs the first "weapon" he can find. That is perhaps not a weapon.

Madam Ford   Nay, good sweet husband.

She offers one of her shoes.

Use this!

Enter **Madam Page** *and* **Falstaff** *disguised as an old man. He really tries to play it up but he's clearly bad at it.*

Falstaff (*in a bad old man voice*)   I'm an old man. I'm such an old man.

Ford   Tuh!

He attempts to hit **Falstaff** *with the shoe.*

Ford   Out of my door, you witch, you devil, you baggage, you polecat, you runnion, out, out! I'll conjure you, I'll fortune-tell you!

There is a not-so-exciting scuffle as **Falstaff** *is able to evade any hits from* **Ford** *before he runs out and exits.*

Falstaff   Out of the way, fam! An old ass man coming through!

Madam Page   Are you not ashamed? I think you have killed the poor man.

Madam Ford   Nay, he will do it. 'Tis a goodly credit for you!

Pastor Evans   By yea and no, I think the man is the old witch doctor of Benin indeed. Yet . . . his feet were moving fast-fast for an old man . . . (*Thinks.*)

Ford   Will you follow, gentlemen? I beseech you, follow, see but the issue of my jealousy. If I cry out thus upon no trail, never trust me when I open again.

Ford *exits to the back of the laundromat.*

Page   Let's obey his humor a little further. Come, gentlemen.

Page, **Caius**, **Pastor Evans**, *and* **Shallow** *follow after* **Ford**. *The wives start to laugh once they are alone.*

Madam Page   Trust me, he beat him most pitifully.

Madam Ford   Nay, by the Mass, that he did not: He beat him most unpitifully, I thought.

Madam Page   I'll have the cudgel hallowed and hung over the altar: It has done meritorious service.

Madam Ford   What do you think? May we, with the warrant of womanhood and the witness of a good conscience, pursue him with any further revenge?

Madam Page   The spirit of wantonness is sure scared out of him.

Madam Ford   Shall we tell our husbands how we have served him?

Madam Page   Yes, by all means, if it be but to scrape the memories out of your husband's brains.

Madam Ford   I'll warrant they'll have him publicly shamed.

Madam Page   Come, to the forge with it, then shape it. We need to strike while the iron is hot.

They exit.

Scene Two

Falstaff *pops up somewhere in the audience, looking for shelter.*

Falstaff (*to audience*)   Hey . . . Yeah. . . Didn't think you'd see me back here, did you?. . . Me neither! Ain't this about a . . . (*Muffled cursed word.*) Man . . . It's been a long, hard year y'all. Couldn't go to the clubs. Couldn't hit up the bars. Liquor stores was closed all early. Been stuck in the house just eating snacks. Watching Netflix. Bored outta my Got-damned mind! (*To an audience member.*) You know what I'm talking about . . . So can you blame me for tryna get with Madam Page and Madam Ford? You know? Those are some MERRY WIVES! You feel me? Just as fine as they wanna be. (*To an audience member.*) Beautiful, right? Yeah see. They're about to get you in trouble too! Don't even think about it! Gonna have you stuck out here like me! Nowhere to go. Nowhere to hide. (*Thinks about hiding under the stage.*) Nah, them raccoons down there don't play. Now they got me out here . . . In the middle of the park . . . Dressed like some ol' Black Dumbledore (*Thinks he hears someone coming— runs.*) Oh shoot, someone's coming![5]

Scene Three

Enter **Page**, **Ford**, **Madam Page**, **Madam Ford**, **Doctor Caius**, **Shallow**, *and* **Pastor Evans**.

Madam Ford   . . . And after that, Chiagozie rolled him into the river! And that is what we did to catch him.

---

[5]   Note: For future productions, there is a permissible improv encouraged here to fit the type of the stage, theatre or venue the production is being performed in. Thank you.

Pastor Evans   That is . . . the most impressive plan I've ever heard.

Page   And did he send you both these letters at an instant?

Madam Page   Within a quarter of an hour.

Ford   Pardon me, wife. Henceforth do what you want.

I rather will suspect the sun with cold

Than you with wantonness. Now doth thy honor stand, In him that was of late an heretic, as firm as faith.

Madam Page (*rolls her eyes, thinks on it*)   Okay fine. I forgive you, you fool.

Ford *and* **Madam Ford** *hug it out.*

Page   Fine. Fine. Fine. No more.

Be not as extreme in submission as in offense.

But let our plot go forward. Let our wives

Yet once again, to make us public sport,

Appoint a meeting with this portly fellow,

Where we may take him and disgrace him for it.

Ford   There is no better way than that they spoke of.

Page   How, to send him word they'll meet him in the park at midnight? Fie, fie, he'll never come.

Pastor Evans   You say he has been thrown in the rivers, and has been grievously beaten as an old man. I think there should be terrors in him, that he should not come.

Doctor Caius   So think I too.

Madam Ford   Devise but how you'll use him when he comes And let us two devise to bring him thither.

Madam Page   There is an old tale goes that Abeeku[6] the Hunter,

---

[6]"Ah-bay-eh-coo".

Sometime a keeper here in the park,

Doth all the summertime, at still midnight,

Walk round about an oak, with great ragged horns,

And there he blasts the tree, and takes the wild animals,

And makes a drink out of their blood and shakes a chain

In a most hideous and dreadful manner.

You have heard of such a spirit.

Page   Why, yet there want not many that do fear In deep of night to walk by this Abeeku's oak.

But what of this?

Madam Ford   Marry now, this should be our plan:

That Falstaff meet us at the oak tree,

Disguised like Abeeku, with huge horns on his head.

Shallow   Well, let it not be doubted but he'll come.

Page   And in this shape; when you have brought him thither, What shall be done with him? What is your plot?

Madam Page   That likewise have we thought upon, and thus:

Three or four we'll dress

Like spirits,

Traditional bright tapers on their heads

And rattles in their hands. Upon a sudden,

As Falstaff, she, and I are newly met,

Let them from forth a sawpit rush at once

With disorienting song. 'Pon their sight,

We two in great amazedness will fly.

Then let them all encircle him about,

And, spirit-like, to pinch the unclean fool,

And ask him why, that hour of spirit revel,

In their so sacred paths he dares to tread

In shape profane.

Madam Ford   Until he tells the truth,

Let the supposed spirits pinch him sound

And burn him with their tapers.

You know, to scare him good, o!

Madam Page   The truth being known,

We'll all present ourselves, dishorn the spirit,

And mock him home.

Ford   Eh-heh! That will be excellent.

Madam Page   My Anne shall be among the spirits, Finely attired in a mask of white.

Page   That I will go buy— (*Aside.*) and in that time Shall Slender steal my Anne away,

And marry her.—Go, send to Falstaff straight.

Pastor Evans   Let us about it.

Page, **Ford**, **Pastor Evans**, **Doctor Caius**, *and* **Shallow** *exit.*

Madam Page   Go, Sista Ford,

Send now-now to Johnny Falstaff to know his mind.

Madam Ford *exits.*

Madam Page   I'll speak to Caius: He has my good will,

And none but he, to marry my daughter.

That Slender, though well landed, is an idiot—

And he my husband best of all affects.

The doctor is well moneyed, and his friends

All powerful. He, none but he, shall have her,

Though twenty thousand worthier come to crave her.

She exits.

Scene Four

Enter **Falstaff**. *He sits on the stoop of his building.*

Falstaff   I would all the world might be deceived, for I have been deceived and beaten too. If it should come to the ear of everyone how I have been transformed and how my transformation has been washed and cudgeled they would melt me out of my fat drop by drop. I warrant they would whip me with their fine wits till I were as lifeless as a dried pear. Well, if I were in better shape, I would repent.

Enter **Mama Quickly**.

Falstaff   Now, where did you come from?

Mama Quickly   From the two parties, forsooth.

Falstaff   The devil take one party, and his dam the other, and so they shall be both bestowed. I have suffered more for their sakes, more than the villainous inconstancy of man's disposition is able to bear.

Mama Quickly   And Madam Ford and Madam Page—have they not suffered?

Falstaff   And what about me?! I was like to be apprehended for an old man witch doctor. But that my admirable dexterity of wit, my counterfeiting the action of an old man, delivered me.

Mama Quickly   Sir, here is a letter that explains things somewhat.

She gives him a paper.

Let me speak with you in your chamber, you shall hear how things go, and, I warrant, to your content. Good hearts, what ado here is to bring you together!

Falstaff   Come up to my chamber.

They exit.

Scene Five

Enter **Fenton** *and* **Pistol***.*

Pistol   Talk not to me. My mind is heavy, Fenton.

Fenton   Yet hear me speak, Pistol. Assist me in my purpose,

I'll give you a hundred dollars more than your loss.

Pistol *stops. Money talks.*

Pistol   Alright, I will hear you and I will, at the least, Keep your counsel.

Fenton   From time to time I have made it known to you

The dear love I bear to fair Anne Page,

Who loves me too.—

So far forth as herself might be her chooser—

Even to my wish.

Tonight at Abeeku's oak, around twelve and one o'clock,

Must my sweet Anne be presented as a Spirit,

In which disguise,

Her father has commanded her to slip

Away with Slender to immediately marry.

Pistol   Wow . . .

Fenton   And she has consented.

Pistol   Whaaaaat?!

Fenton   And it gets worse. Her mother, who doesn't care for Slender And is firm for Doctor Caius, has appointed

That he shall likewise shuffle her away,

To the church, where a pastor attends,

And straight marry her.

Now thus it rests:

Her father means she shall be masked in blue

And when Slender sees his time, he shall

Take her by the hand and bid her to go with him.

Her mother has intended for her to go with the doctor.

And they will all be masked and vizarded—

And when the doctor spies his vantage ripe, he will

Pinch her by the hand, and Anne will go with him.

Pistol   Which means she to deceive, Father or Mother?

Fenton   Both . . .

Pistol *is confused but quickly gets it.*

Pistol   To go along with you!   **Fenton**   To go along with me!

Fenton   And here it rests: that you'll get the pastor

To stay for me at church, between twelve and one,

And, in the lawful name of marrying,

To give our hearts united ceremony.

Pistol (*gives* **Fenton** *back his money*)   Bring you Anne Page, you shall not lack a pastor.

Fenton   So shall I evermore be bound to thee!

They exit.

Act Five

Scene One

Falstaff *escorts* **Mama Quickly** *out of his apartment.*

Falstaff   Prithee, no more prattling. Go, I'll hold: This is the THIRD time-I hope good luck lies in odd numbers. Away, go! They say there is divinity in odd numbers, either in nativity, chance, or death. Away!

Mama Quickly   I'll provide you a chain and I'll do what I can to get you a pair of horns.

Falstaff   Away, I say! Time wears.

They exit.

Scene Two

Enter **Page**, **Shallow**, *and* **Slender**.

Page   Here: We'll couch in the ditch till we see the lights of our spirits. Remember, son Slender, my daughter—

Slender   Look here, I have spoken with her, and we have a codeword for how to know one another. I'll go to her, where she'll be in a blue mask and cry "sugar," and she'll cry "cane," and by that we'll know one another.

Shallow   That's good too. But what needs either your "sugar" or her "cane"? The blue mask will decipher her well enough.—It has struck ten o'clock.

Page   The night is dark: Lights and spirits will become it well. Heaven prosper our sport! No man means evil but the devil, and we shall know him by his horns. Let's go.

They exit.

Scene Three

Enter **Madam Page**, **Madam Ford**, *and* **Doctor Caius**.

Madam Page   Doctor Caius, my daughter is masked in white: When you see your time, take her by the hand, away with her to the church, and dispatch it quickly. Go into the park.—We two must go together.

Doctor Caius   I know vat I have to do. Adieu.

Caius *exits.*

Madam Page   My husband will not rejoice so much at the abuse of Falstaff as he will chafe at the doctor's marrying my daughter. But it doesn't matter. Better a little chiding than a great deal of heartbreak.

Madam Ford   Where is Anne now, and her troop of spirits, and the silly Pastor?

Madam Page   They are all couched in a pit hard by Abeeku's oak.

Madam Ford   This cannot choose but amaze him.

Madam Page   Against lewd people and their lechery, Those that betray them do no treachery.

Madam Ford   It's almost time. To the oak. To the oak!

They exit.

Scene Four

Enter **Pastor Evans** *and others disguised as spirits.*

Pastor Evans   Come, spirits, come, come, gather! Remember your parts. Be bold, I pray you. Follow me, and when I give the signal, do as I bid you.

They exit.

Scene Five

Enter **Falstaff***, wearing a buck's head and a chain.*

Falstaff   The clock hath struck twelve, the minute draws on.

Enter **Madam Page** *and* **Madam Ford**.

Falstaff   Who comes here? My doe?

Madam Ford   Johnny? Art thou there, my deer, my male deer?

Falstaff   My doe with the black short tail! Let the sky rain
plantains, let it thunder to melodious tunes. Let there come a
tempest of provocation, and I will shelter me here.

He embraces her.

Madam Ford   Madam Page is come with me, sweetheart.

Falstaff   Ooo! Okay! Divide me like a roasted goat, each a large
portion. I will keep my sides to myself, my shoulders for the fellow
of this walk,—and my horns I give to your husbands. Am I a
woodman, ha? Why, now is Cupid a child of conscience: He makes
restitution. As I am a true spirit, welcome.

A noise of horns and unfamiliar sounds are heard.

Madam Page   Eh-eh, what is that noise?

Madam Ford   Heaven forgive our sins!

Falstaff   Uh . . . What should this be?

Madam Ford and **Madam Page**   Let's go! Let's go!

The two women run off. Enter **Mama Quickly**.

Mama Quickly (*as Spirit Queen*)

West African regionally specific ululations:

Spirits black, gray, green, and white,

You moonshine revelers and shades of night,

You orphan heirs of fixed destiny,

Attend your office and your quality.

Spirits! Spirits! I'm calling to you, o!

Enter **Spirits**.

Falstaff (*aside*)   These are spirits! He that speaks to them shall die.

I'll wink and wait. No man their works must eye.

He crouches down and covers his eyes.

Mama Quickly   Spirits, oh! I call on you, come about. All of the spirits both within and out.

For we've made it through the greatest of storms

And new days of love, joy, and freedom born.

We lived a time where we were pushed inside

Not a hug or held hand was felt worldwide

Now many have joined you spirits above

Honored forever in dignified love

New meaning to life we all understand,

That love is present wherever we land.

Spirits, help guide us in this time anew

Where we recognize the reckoning due

For our hues and lives matter, full stop.

Here in the forefront and not a backdrop.

Call forth those in power to make room now

To do as they've promised and vowed

Now is the time for the reformation

Now is the time to rebuild the nation!

Tonight, dear spirits, we thank you for life

No more pain or hurt of living in strife.

Spirits, spirits! Be with us whenever,

To guide our path, now and forever!

All   To guide our path, now and forever!

Mama Quickly (*to everyone*)   Away, disperse! But till 'tis one o'clock spoke,

Our dance of custom round about the oak.

Pastor Evans (*as a spirit*)   Eh-eh! But stay! I smell a man . . . of the earth.

Falstaff (*aside*)   Heavens defend me from these spirits she's called on.

Slender (*as a spirit, to* **Falstaff**)   Vile worm, thou was overlooked even when you were born.

Mama Quickly (*as Spirit Queen*)   With trial-fire touch me his finger end:

If he be chaste, the flame will back descend

And turn him to no pain; but if he start,

It is the flesh of a corrupted heart.

Slender (*as a spirit*)   A trial!

Spirits   A trial!

A trial!

Pastor Evans (*as a spirit*)   Come! Will this wood take fire?

Some of the other spirits put a fire taper to **Falstaff**.

Falstaff (*terrified*)   Ow, Ow, Ow!

Mama Quickly (*as Spirit Queen*)   Corrupt! Corrupt! And tainted in desire!

Spirit! Get him! Sing a scornful rhyme,

And, as you trip, still pinch him to your time.

Here they pinch him and hiss at him. **Falstaff** *is completely and utterly frightened.*

Spirits (*singing/chanting*)

Pinch him! Pinch him!
Pinch him! Pinch him!
Pinch him! Pinch him!
Pinch him! Pinch him!
Pinch him! Pinch him!
Pinch him! Pinch him!

As the ceremony comes to an end, **Falstaff** *screams in terror. All of the spirits laugh at him as some of them take off their masks.* **Doctor Caius** *runs off with someone masked in white.* **Slender** *runs away with someone who is masked in blue.* **Fenton** *runs off with* **Anne Page**—*both of them masked.* **Falstaff** *pulls off his buck's head, confused.*

Madam Page (*points to the horns*)   See you these, husband? Do not these fair horns

Become the forest better than the town?

Ford (*to* **Falstaff**)   Now, sir, who's a cuckold now? (*Mocking* **Falstaff**.) "Mister Brook, Ford's a knave! A foolish, wittolly, cuck- oldy knave!" (*Laughs.*) "Here are his horns, Mister Brook."

Madam Ford   Johnny, we have had ill luck, we could never meet. But I will never take you for my love again, but I will always count you my deer.

Falstaff (*realizing . . . aside*)   I do begin to perceive that I am made an ass. And these are not spirits. I was three or four times in the thought they were not spirits, and yet the guiltiness of my mind, the sudden surprise of my powers, drove the grossness of the foppery into a received belief, that they were spirits. See now how wit may be made a dummy when it is upon ill employment.

Pastor Evans Falstaff, serve God and leave your desires, and spirits will not haunt you.

Ford Well said, Spirit Evans.

Pastor Evans And, you Mister Ford—leave you your jealousies too, I pray you.

Ford I will never mistrust my wife again, o!

Enter **Slender** *with someone covered in a blue mask.*

Slender Father Page!

Page Son, how now, o! Have you, eh, settled the business?

Slender Settled what? Would I were killed or else!

Page Eh?

Slender I came yonder to marry Anne Page, but somehow, she was not Anne Page. And I kissed the wrong girl! Married the wrong girl! Oh lord! Have I acted unholy?!

Page Upon my life, then, you took the wrong.

Slender What need you tell me that? I think so, when I took another girl for some other girl.

Page Why, this is your own folly. Did not I tell you how you should know my daughter by her garments?

Slender Yes! I went to her, in the blue mask, and cried "sugar" and I thought she cried "cane," and yet it was not Anne, but a post-master's daughter!

She takes off her mask.

But me, I'm happy, oh. Look at her! She's very fine-fine!

He smiles. Can't believe his luck!

Madam Page Kwame, please don't be angry. I knew of your purpose, masked our daughter in white, and indeed she is now with the doctor at the church, and there married.

Enter **Doctor Caius** *with another person in a white mask.*

Doctor Caius (*thrilled!*)   Madam Page!!!! Sank you! Sank you so much!

Madam Page   Oh, good Doctor Caius! Pray you tell me—did you take the one masked in white?

Doctor Caius   I did! And it was un garçon!

The gentleman with the doctor takes off his mask.

Madam Page   What?!

Doctor Caius   I love that you surprise-a me!

He likes his new husband.

You know-a me so vell!

Ford   Well, this is strange. Who hath got the right Anne?

Enter **Fenton** *and* **Anne Page**.

Page   My heart misgives me.—Here comes Fenton.—How now, Fenton? Anne . . . how chance you went not with Slender?

Madam Page   Why went you not with Doctor Caius, Anne?

Fenton   You do amaze her. Hear the truth of it. I—

Anne *interrupts.*

Anne   —Uh, let me . . .

(*To* **Madam Page** *and* **Page**.) Mother, Father; I ask your forgiveness. I know that you wanted all the best for me.

But you'd have married me most shamefully,

Where there was no proportion held in love.

The truth is, she and I, long since contracted,

Are now so sure that nothing can dissolve us.

Fenton   The offense is holy that I have committed,

And this deceit loses the name of craft,

Of disobedience, or unduteous title,

Since therein I do shun

A thousand irreligious cursed hours

Which forced marriage would have brought upon her.

Anne   And I wanted to marry for love

 Fenton   Yes . . . for love.

Ford (*to* **Page** *and* **Madam Page**)   Stand not amazed. Here is no remedy.

In love the heavens themselves do guide the state.

Page   Well, what remedy?!

What cannot be eschewed, must be embraced.

(*To* **Fenton**.) Welcome to the family, o!

Page *hugs* **Fenton** *and* **Anne**. *Everyone applauds.*

Madam Page   Well, we must muse no further.—Fenton and my darling Anne,

Heaven give you many, merry, merry days!

(*To* **Page**.) Husband, let's all go home

And laugh this sport over.

Falstaff *clears his throat.*

Madam Page   Even Falstaff can come. Because tonight, o! Tonight, we party!

They laugh and exit. Curtain call: a big old African wedding celebration!

End of play.

Nollywood Dreams

World Premiere at the MCC Theater, 2021
Artistic Directors: Robert LuPone, Bernard Telsey, &
William Cantler
Executive Director: Blake West

Nollywood Dreams was developed by the Cherry Lane
Mentor Project
(Angelina Fiordellisi, Founding Artistic Director) in April 2017

Nollywood Dreams was developed with the support of
New York Stage & Film and Vassar's Powerhouse season,
Summer 2016

Characters

Note: All characters are of West African descent and are to be played by Black and/or African actors. Thank you.

Ayamma (I-YAH-MAH) **Okafor** (OAK-AH-FOUR)—*twenties / early thirties—aspiring Nigerian film actress with raw talent. Works as a travel agent/secretary at her parents' office. She is a big dreamer and hopes for a better life for herself as a famous actress.*

Dede (DEE-DEE) **Okafor** (OAK-AH-FOUR)—*twenties / thirties—Ayamma's older sister. She works (if you call it working) at her parents' travel agency. She loves all things pop culture: talk shows, soap operas, and celebrities. She's incredibly close to Ayamma and also serves as her little sister's truth teller when necessary.*

Gbenga (BENG-GAH) **Ezie** (EHH-ZEE)—*thirties—Rising Nigerian film director. Is known for his wealth and his famous education having studied in America. He harbors devastating secrets to his success.*

Wale (WHA-LAY) **Owusu** (OH-WOO-SUE)—*twenties / thirties—Nigeria's hottest rising star. Every woman wants him and every man man wants to be him, but rarely do people ever get to know him or his story. Quietly confident. Everything about him is smooth.*

Fayola (FAYE-OH-LA) **Ogunleye** (OH-GOON-LAY-YAY)—*thirties—commonly referred to as "The Nigerian Halle Berry with Tina Turner Legs"—she was, for a time, a bonafide Nollywood star. She is incredibly beautiful, sexy, talented and she knows it. Her career took a hard blow because of some personal decisions and she is now desperate for the spotlight again.*

Adenikeh (AH-DEN-KNEE-KAY)—*late thirties / early forties—The Nigerian "Oprah Winfrey".*

Television Announcer/Movie Trailer Voice—*twenties and/or older; male—is the voice behind the television commercials and the movie trailer for "The Comfort Zone."*

Setting

Lagos, Nigeria—Early 1990s.

Note from the Playwright

In the early 1990s, Nigeria, in the midst of economic and political turmoil, saw an explosion of independent films being produced. Many of the themes of these films dealt with love or family issues but were layered in subtext about the political strife/temperature of the country. In one very popular film (my personal favorite, actually) a man falls in love with two women: a commoner and the daughter of the president. Veiled as a classic love triangle, we follow the main character's dilemma as he tries to choose between living like the upper crust of Nigeria or a life of squalor with his (perhaps, true love) the commoner. Because of the political unrest at the time, this was a common choice for many Nigerians—join the military and live the life of a wealthy general or struggle to pay your bills as the government unjustly siphoned your wages. Thus, our main character was telling the story of the sad duality that existed in Nigeria at the time: live like the rich or suffer like the poor—there is no middle. One could say the same about America, but I digress.

The quality of Nollywood films of this time were usually low budget, shot with very limited takes based on a loose script/outline that actors mostly improv over. Mainly released on video cassettes and DVDs, Nollywood films were sold in marketplaces for a relatively low cost and, soon, they quickly became high in demand. By the early 2000s, the Nollywood market had exploded with new films being produced and sold so quickly that the Nollywood film industry became (and still remains) the second highest producing film industry in the world ("Bollywood" is first and the American film industry, "Hollywood," is third.)

These were the films of my youth. I watched many of them while getting my hair braided at my aunt's salon or the ones that would play in an endless loop at my grandmother's home, Ghana, where I spent many summers. I wanted to write a love letter to this amazing and uniquely specific expression of African artistry that not everyone will understand, but I hope will come to appreciate its existence. *Nollywood Dreams* is my imagining of what it was like when this incredible film industry was beginning to take the world by storm, o!

Dedicated to: Saheem Ali . . . For always being my "comfort zone." :)

Scene One: Okafor Travel Agency

Early afternoon at the agency. **Dede** *hurries to sit in front of the television with a batch of cookies and a cup of warm tea. She is nearly bursting with excitement as the television announcer is heard.*

Television Announcer (O.S/V.O) (*West African accent*)   Stay Tuned! Coming up next is a brand new episode of *Adenikeh*, where she interviews famous Nollywood film director—Gbenga Ezie! You won't want to miss it!

Dede (*singing along with the television, off key—smooth jazz kind of sound*)   "Adenikeh! Bringing love into your home!"

As **Dede** *eats her cookies,* **Ayamma** *enters the travel agency and hurriedly rushes passed* **Dede** *to the television.*

Ayamma   Has *Adenikeh* started yet?!

Dede   Eh-eh, watch it! You will spill my tea.

Ayamma   Oh sorry. I'm just so excited!

Dede   What is it, eh? Making all this fuss . . . What is this book you have?

Ayamma   This is the script for that new Gbenga Ezie movie I was telling you about.

I heard from some friends that he is having an open casting call, so I went down to his studios and picked up a copy of the script!

Dede (*eating cookies*)   Okay . . . So, what are you going to do with that?

Ayamma   Audition!

Small pause. **Dede** *chews.*

Dede   . . . Eh?

Ayamma   Come on, Dede, you know that my true passion is acting.

Dede   Ayamma, are we still on this? I thought it was clear that you are . . . not . . . Good.

Ayamma   Excuse me? Don't you remember how amazing I was in that church play when I was eight years old?

Dede   Yes . . . And you were not good then. It's only we were in church, we couldn't be honest.

Ayamma   Well, it doesn't matter. This is my calling—I can feel it. And I am perfect for this part! It's like I always say, all you have to have is good looks. The director will do the rest.

Dede   Mmm, hmm. A director. Not a magician!

Ayamma   Dede, this could be my big break! Can you imagine? Your little sister . . . My name in the lights . . . Ayamma Okafor starring as "Comfort Aleshinloye" in *The Comfort Zone.*

Dede   De what?

Ayamma   That's the name of the movie. There was a whole interview the director did in the newspaper about it. It's the 90s now—I'm telling you Nigerian movies are getting bigger and bigger. They think it might even crossover into America!

Small pause. **Dede** *chews.*

Dede   Ayamma . . . I don't mean to pop your bubble sky dreams or whatever, but if this movie is going to be "so big," why would they put some nobody like you in it?

Ayamma   You are not going to make jokes when I tell you the best part: Guess who is playing the leading man?

Dede   Eddie Murphy?

Ayamma   No . . . Think on it.

Dede   I mean, he was very good in *Coming to America.*

Ayamma   No, Dede . . . It's Wale Owusu.

Dede   Wale Owusu?!

Ayamma   Yes.

Dede   As in my future husband?

Ayamma   Yes!

Dede   You mean, someone is going to PAY you for a chance to touch Wale Owusu?

Ayamma   Not just touch . . . Kiss him!

Dede   EHHH! We have to get in this movie!

Ayamma   I know!

Dede   So . . . how much does it pay?

Ayamma (*deep breath*)   Two thousand dollars.

Dede   Dollars? He's paying in American money?! How much is that in Naira?

Ayamma   Three . . . hundred . . . thousand . . . Naira.

Dede   For one movie?

Ayamma *nods her head excitedly.*

Dede   Ayamma, if we do enough of these movies . . .

WE ARE GOING TO BE RICH!

Ayamma   I know! But, let me get the part first!

Dede   Okay, okay.

They momentarily calm, but then get excited all over again.

Ayamma *and* **Dede**   Ahhhh!

Dede   I just cannot believe this!

Ayamma   I know, me too! But I need to focus. My audition is in one week and I want to be off book by then.

Dede   Which book?

Ayamma   OFF book. It is how American actors say "memorize."

Dede   These people. As if learning English is not hard enough.

Ayamma (*gives* **Dede** *the script*)   Okay, so you're going read all of the lines that say "James."

Dede (*smitten*)   Is that who Wale is going to play?

Ayamma   Yes. And I'm going to read for "Comfort." Let's just go ahead and read the scene for cold—(*proud of herself*)—that means for the first time—and then we'll go back.

Dede (*chews cookie*)   Okay.

Ayamma   But first, let me warm up.

Ayamma *begins to do her version of an actor warm up. It's odd—especially to* **Dede**.

Ayamma   Okay, I'm ready. (*Melodramatic*) "But why didn't you tell me?
All this time I've been here waiting for you to come back to me. Only to find out you have a wife . . . A family . . . and a job that you cannot leave."

Dede (*chews, barely invested*)   "Oh Comfort. If only you know how much I want to be with you."

Ayamma   "With me? Oh please. Actions speak louder than words, James!"

Dede   "You don't know how many times my heart beats for you when I lay in bed at night. And how I dream of being your liver."

Ayamma (*breaking character*)   Lover.

Dede   Fine, "Lover." Ah! But why are these words so small? I can barely see.

Ayamma   Dede please. Just pay attention. I want to be perfect.

Dede (*sucks teeth*)   Whatever. But as soon as *Adenikeh* comes on, I'm done.

Ayamma Fine. Where I was? Ah yes . . . (*Back in character.*)
"Well if you dream of us being together, why don't you just leave
your wife? Be with me. Let us stay here and live our lives together.
Forever!"

Dede "You don't understand . . . It is so complicated. I just don't
know what to do." (*Sucks teeth.*) It doesn't sound complicated to
me. He is going to leave his wife, children and green card in
America to come here and live with you in some run-down flat in
Lagos? This movie is stupid.

Ayamma (*snatching the script back from* **Dede**) It's not stupid.
It's about love.
What would you know about that anyway?

Dede Eh-eh! Much more than you, Ayamma! Like the love I
have for Wale Owusu! It's strong, oh! And that is the only reason I
will buy this movie . . . Oh and the money we will get.

Ayamma Eh, I will get.

Dede Yeah, yeah, I'll give you some too.

They laugh a bit.

Ayamma Aww man, Dede, if I book this, I don't know what I'd
do! Finally leaving this travel agency and living my REAL dream.

Dede (*wasn't listening*) Oh, speaking of which, Daddy has a big
account with some students from Europe and he wants to make
sure you handle it.

Ayamma Ah, why can't you do it?

Dede Well, first above all, you are the only one of us who knows
how to use these crazy computers. And anyway, I'm older than
you. I have other things to do.

Ayamma Like what? Sit in Mary's hair salon all day and talk
about what is happening on *Days of Our Lives?*

Dede Eh-eh! Where else am I supposed to watch it? We only get
two clear channels on this thing. I can't miss it! On the next

episode, Marlena is finally going to escape from Stefano's prison lair . . . It's going to be good.

Ayamma   I think it's best if I spend my time working on this script, thank you.

Dede *offers* **Ayamma** *a cookie.*

Dede   Want a cookie?

Ayamma   No, no. I need to watch my figure.

Dede   Oh please. (*Distracted by the TV.*) Ooh, ooh, ooh! Shhh, it's on now!

Dede *turns up the volume.*

The "theme music" to Adenikeh *begins to play.*

> **Adenikeh Theme Song**
> *WHEN YOUR SPIRIT IS SAD AND YOU'VE GIVEN UP AND*
>   *YOU*
> *DON'T KNOW WHERE TO GO*
> *DON'T GET DOWN, TURN AROUND,*
> *PICK UP THAT REMOTE*
> *AND TUNE INTO YOUR FAVORITE SHOW!*
> *ADENIKEH!*
> *BRINGING LOVE INTO YOUR HOME.*

Ayamma *and* **Dede** (*singing along, off key*)   "Adenikeh! Bringing love into your home!"

Adenikeh (O.S/V.O)   Hello everyone and welcome to *Adenikeh.* Thank you for letting me bring love into your home.

Light claps from the audience are heard.

And today, I'm bringing you more than just love—as I will be interviewing the hottest director in what critics around the world are now calling the Nigerian Film Industry—"Nollywood." His new film, *The Comfort Zone* is slated to be released on home video later this year.

Ayamma   That's the movie I was telling you about.

Dede   Oh that's what you were talking about.

Adenikeh   Audience please help me welcome, internationally award-winning director, GBENGA EZIE!

Dede *and* **Ayamma** *cheer and clap along with the audience as the stage transitions into:*

Scene Two: *Adenikeh* TV Studio

Adenikeh *is the midst of an interview with* **Gbenga Ezie**. *The* Adenikeh *theme song fades out. Light claps from the audience.*

Gbenga   Oh, thank you, Adenikeh. It is always wonderful to be on your show.

Adenikeh   Happy to have you. I think the last time you were here, you were about to head off to America.

Gbenga   Yes that's right. I spent a few years in New York before moving to Los Angeles and working in Hollywood.

Adenikeh   And tell me, was your time there the inspiration to bring a new kind of show business model to Nigeria?

Gbenga   Yes, it is important to me to make Nollywood as competitive a market as Hollywood is. Don't get me wrong— America is amazing, but I felt so constricted over there.

Adenikeh   Mmm. Interesting. How so?

Gbenga   Well, I would go into these meetings and they all wanted me to write movies about what they assumed was my experience. War. Poverty.

Adenikeh (*chiming in*)   Eh hehn. Sadness. Famine . . . These people.

Gbenga   Exactly! There I was, at the epicenter of entertainment and I realized—these people have no vision.

Adenikeh   Wow.

Gbenga   So, I had this script that I had been working on and everyone wanted it! Martin Scorsese, Steven Spielberg—all of them—and finally in my last studio meeting, I said, "You know what, Mr. Coppola, I think I am going to take *my* script back to *my* homeland."

Adenikeh   Amazing! And you weren't just in Hollywood. You spent some time on the east coast where I'm sure you met quite a few characters at NYU. New York University—for those of you who don't know—is one of the most prestigious schools in America and Gbenga received a full scholarship into the Film program.

Gbenga   Uh . . . yes. Yes, I did. And I met all sorts of amazing people who helped me further my career along. In fact, that is where I started writing the first draft of *The Comfort Zone*.

Adenikeh   Yes! And I think it's safe to say that we all can't wait to see it! Aren't we all anxiously awaiting to see Wale Owusu on screen again, ladies?

The audience cheers, claps and whistles.

Adenikeh   So, as I understand, this film is about a man struggling to find where his true love lies: with his wife in America or his Nigerian love, Comfort.

Gbenga   Yes. It is an intriguing story of a very complicated love triangle.

Adenikeh   You know, Gbenga, there are rumors out there that this film may just, in fact, be based on your own life?

The audience "oohs and ahhs" with intrigue.

Gbenga (*laughs*)   No, no. I assure you, it has nothing to do with me.

Adenikeh   I'm just joking. But seriously—the issues you're addressing in this film are poignant. Sham marriages. Internet scams. Wire fraud. These kinds of things are bringing shame to our people. Don't you agree?

Gbenga   Umm, yes, they are. And sadly, I too was tempted to go down that road.

The audience gasps in shock.

Adenikeh (*dramatic . . . Shocked*)   Really?!

Gbenga   Yes, but thankfully, I uh . . . chose differently.

The audience is relieved.

Adenikeh   And so are we! Look at you—you're about to change the world!

Gbenga   I hope so.

Adenikeh   But for now, you are about to change the life of one very lucky young actress with your Open Casting Call for the lead role of "Comfort!"

Gbenga   That's right. I want to see any and all talent that we have here in Nigeria. So if you are eighteen years and older and have an interest in being an actress, please head down to my Nollywood Dreams Movie Studio and sign up to audition!

The audience cheers loudly with excitement.

Adenikeh   Amazing. I can't wait to see who that lucky young lady is . . . Okay, it is time for us to take a short break, but we will be back in just a moment. Do not change from this program.

The audience claps as the Adenikeh *theme song plays out. A camera operator is heard saying, "And cut. Two minutes until we're back."* **Gbenga** *and* **Adenikeh** *relax a bit, sip water, etc.*

Adenikeh   So this *Comfort Zone* movie sounds very exciting, eh?

Gbenga   Oh yes. I'm hoping it will do very well.

Adenikeh   Me too . . . You know, I used to do a bit of acting myself.

Gbenga   Oh yeah?

Adenikeh   I mean, it's been a long time, but I'm sure it's like riding a bike you know?

Gbenga   Exactly. Talent is talent.

Adenikeh   Mmm hmmm . . . and you know . . . That *Color Purple* thing did wonders for Oprah, so you know, just think of sister Adenikeh when you're writing your next big film, eh?

Gbenga (*nervous laughter*)   Oh, sure. Of course.

Offstage a camera man is heard "and we're back in 5. 4. 3. 2 . . ."
the Adenikeh *theme music plays as the stage transitions into:*

Scene Three: Okafor Travel Agency Office

Dede *and* **Ayamma** *are at their desks.* **Dede** *sits with her feet propped up, sipping tea, eating a snack of some sort and reading a magazine.* **Ayamma** *is going over her lines silently—but full of expression. The phone rings for a long while before* **Dede** *begrudgingly picks it up.*

Dede (*into phone*)   Thank you for calling Okafor Travels. This is Dede. How may I help you? (*Listens.*) Ah yes, just one moment. (*To* **Ayamma**.)

It's for you.

Ayamma   Who is it?

Dede   I don't know. Someone who wants to book a flight.

Ayamma (*sucks teeth . . . picks up call*)   Thank you for holding. This is Ayamma, how may I help you? (*Listens.*) Eh, no mam. We do not offer safari packages. (*Listens.*) Eh, the Serengeti is not in Nigeria . . . No, no—wrong part of Africa. Sorry. (*Sucks teeth as she hangs up.*) These white people.

Dede   Africa is a country to them, you know that.

Ayamma   Well I cannot be bothered with their foolishness today. I've only got one hour left to perfect

Dede   "This audition."

Ayamma   This audition.

Dede   Yes, yes, yes, we know. I swear, I cannot wait until it is over because I'm so sick of hearing about it.

Ayamma   Pardon?

Dede   Ah, Ayamma, but it's all you've been talking about. Me, I cannot even sleep without dreaming about your lines. (*More.*)

(*Mocking.*) "Oh, James, you've betrayed me. You've hurt me, Oh, oh, oh!"

Ayamma   I can see the jealousy written all over your face.

Dede   Oh please. My only goal right now is to get to Wale. Chai! If you get this movie, you have no idea! Me, I will be on set everyday and it will only be a matter of time before Wale takes one look at me and he will just collapse. 'Cause his body will not be able to withstand the powerful chemistry we will have. I'm telling you!

Dede *continues to read.* **Ayamma** *has, just a bit, "Gone Nollywood" already.*

Ayamma   Dede please! If I—WHEN I get this movie, you won't be able to just hang around. The movie set is a sacred space where very powerful art is being created. You know, I started reading *Acting in Film* and Michael Caine says that true acting—

Dede (*reading*)   Hey . . . hey did you see this?

Ayamma   Dede, I don't care about that silly village gossip.

Dede   Okay, so it's just gossip that Mr. Ezie is considering another girl for the role of "Comfort."

Ayamma   What?!

Dede (*reading out loud*)   "Anticipation is building as Gbenga Ezie compiles his list of actors for his new film *The Comfort Zone*. Word has been spreading rapidly that Mr. Ezie is strongly considering former child star turned Nollywood darling, Fayola

Ogunleye for the lead role of 'Comfort.' Commonly regarded as the 'Nigerian Halle Berry with Tina Turner legs,' her casting would mark the second time Fayola and Wale would work together according to some Olofofo birds in the know. We'll have to wait and see if Mr. Ezie will make lightning strike again."

Ayamma   First above all, she looks nothing like Halle Berry.

Dede   That is true. I would say more like a close relative . . . But the "Tina Turner legs?" Dead on.

Ayamma   Ah! But that is not right. How could he say that he wants fresh faces, but would "strongly consider" her?

Dede (*sarcasm . . . and eating*)   Oh, but I thought you don't care about silly village gossip?

Ayamma   I don't! . . . So what if he is letting Fayola audition? Good for her. I mean, honestly, who is she?

Dede   Yes, I know it. She just comes from a wealthy family . . . Men are always going crazy over her . . . She has already been in several films . . . AND she knows Wale . . . but hey, you never know. Maybe, he'll skip over her and give you—a modest, homely, village girl—a chance.

Ayamma *stares a hole into* **Dede***'s head.*

Dede   You want me to put a curse on her?

Ayamma   Dede, you know your curses never work.

Dede   Maybe this will be the one.

The phone rings.

Ayamma   Whatever. I'm leaving.

Dede   Where are you going?

Ayamma   I need to handle some business before I go downtown.

Ayamma *begins to hurriedly gather her things.*

Dede   Oh, getting a new, hot, outfit at the market? You are nervous now, eh?

Ayamma   No.

Ayamma *continues to collect her things. The phone continues to ring.*

Dede   Eh-eh! But who is going to answer these phone lines?

Ayamma   Dede, please. Why don't you try doing some work for a change?

Dede   I do plenty of work around here . . . And anyway, you are supposed to be handling the business. You know I don't know how to work these crazy computers.

Ayamma (*sighs*)   Can you just do me this one favor? Please? Sista?

Dede (*sucks teeth*)   Fine. But bring me a large pack of ginger cookies from the market.

Ayamma (*quickly*)   Ah, you do not need any more cookies.

Dede   You say what?

Ayamma   Nothing. Fine. I've got to go. Wish me luck!

Ayamma *rushes out. The phone continues to ring.*

Dede (*finally answering*)   Thank you for calling Okafor Travels. This is Dede. How may I help you? (*Listens.*) Ehh! Mary! How are you? Oh, fine, fine.

The other phone line begins to ring.

Dede (*ignoring the ring*)   Yes, I have time to talk. What's happening with you? (*Listens.*) That woman came into your salon again?! Is she still wearing that blonde wig? (*Laughs.*) It does look like a coconut tree!

Lights shift.

Scene Four: *Adenikeh* **TV Studio**

Adenikeh *is the midst of an interview with* **Fayola Ogunleye.**

Adenikeh   And we're back with our candid interview with Nollywood darling, Fayola Ogunleye.

Applause from the audience.

Fayola   Thank you so much, Adenikeh.

Adenikeh   Fayola, in the press you are commonly referred to as the "Nigerian Halle Berry—"

Fayola   "With Tina Turner legs."

Adenikeh   Uh, yes. How do you feel about being the apple of men's affections and the envy of all women?

Fayola   Well, I don't know if I am all of that. Honestly, I am just happy to still be working in this business for nearly twenty years.

Adenikeh   Yes, many of us remember you as the lovable younger sister Chioma in the hit television series *Family Comes First*.

Fayola   That was a wonderful time in my life.

Adenikeh   You were once the "go to" actress for many popular projects, so, we were surprised when you decided to leave Nigeria and pursue a career in America some years ago. What was the meaning of this?

Fayola   Honestly . . . I was in love.

Light "Awwws" from the audience.

Fayola   My boyfriend at the time had an opportunity to go to America and asked me to come with him.

Adenikeh   And your love for him did not allow you to say no?

Fayola   He promised me the world and well, I guess you can say I'm a bit of a romantic because I believed him.

Adenikeh   But he did not give you the world, did he?

Fayola   No. Things got . . . a bit . . . complicated.

Adenikeh   Mmm. I understand. And since we are speaking candidly, it is common knowledge that the last few films that you have starred in have not fared well.

Fayola (*under breath*)   Oh okay . . . we're talking about that. . .

Adenikeh   Do you believe that your time away from the spotlight here in Nigeria is the cause of you of losing your fan base?

Some "oohs" from the audience.

Fayola   It is the nature of this business, Adenikeh. Some movies do well and others don't. But I am working on some new, exciting projects now and I have a feeling that things will go my way. Trust me the fans will be very excited.

Adenikeh   Yes, we have heard some rumblings of you perhaps reuniting on screen with the handsome Wale Owusu.

The audience "hoots and whistles" at the thought of Wale Owusu.

Fayola (*over the cheering*)   Oh, so you all like to see that, eh?!

More cheers from the crowd.

Adenikeh   And as for this mystery gentleman—the man who SHATTERED your heart—have you forgiven him for the wishes he did not fulfill?

Fayola   Of course . . . I was taught to forgive others for their mistakes. None of us are perfect.

Adenikeh   Well, I do not know. I would say that if I had legs like yours, I would feel pretty close to perfect.

The audience claps and cheers.

Fayola (*crossing her legs; trying to be coy*)   Oh, Adenikeh, you are too much, oh.

Adenikeh (*to camera*)   Thank you so much, Fayola.

Fayola   No, thank you, Adenikeh!

They hug and **Fayola** *exits—blowing kisses to the audience.*

Adenikeh   Okay, thank you all for joining me today. And be sure to keep tuning in because we have some amazing shows lined up including our next episode where we interview the newest gentleman named Nigeria's Sexiest Man Born! Trust me—you won't want to miss it! I know I won't! See you all soon and thank you for letting me bring love into your home.

The audience claps and cheers as the Adenikeh *theme song plays out.*

Scene Five: Ezie's Nollywood Dreams Studios

Gbenga *and* **Fayola** *exit a studio room and spill into the main lobby laughing and carrying on like old friends.*

Gbenga   Eh, Fayola. I'm so glad that you came in to read for me . . . I have been waiting for us to be able to work together again.

Fayola   Really?

Gbenga   Yes. I kept thinking how perfect you would be for this movie.

Fayola   Well, if I'm so perfect, why have auditions then?

Gbenga   Come now, you know from our time in America, nothing gets people more excited than an open call. You see how good the publicity has been already. I want to ensure this movie will be a hit.

Fayola   Eh! Look at you—"publicity" . . . Using the "Media". . . . Bringing Hollywood to Nollywood, eh?

Gbenga   Well, my time in Los Angeles taught me a lot.

Fayola   I see that. And you've written a great script. "Comfort" is an amazing role.

Gbenga   And I think you would be perfect in it.

Fayola   Thank you . . . I was worried that maybe you were considering me for "Rose." Not that it's not a great part, but come on—I'm no supporting actress.

Gbenga   Of course. If anyone knows that, it is me . . .

They both laugh a bit. Beat.

You know, I was surprised to learn you were back in Nigeria for good. I heard from some people that you stayed in New York?

Fayola   Yeah, I was there for a while. I got connected to a talent agent, so I did a lot of auditions. But it was hard, oh. Always going in for some role like "the best friend," "the maid," or someone who has an attitude problem. Can you believe these parts they have for us?

Gbenga   I know . . . It's a shame.

Fayola   Anyway, I got tired of the business there. So a year ago, I decided to come back home for good. Work on the films that were true to me. You know? Like yours.

Gbenga   Yes, yes—home is where we thrive! We were always told to "get out of Nigeria. Go to the west! There is nothing here for you." But we were here. So what? Were we nothing?

Fayola (*flips hair*)   Well, I certainly am not!

Gbenga (*smiles*)   No . . . you're far from it.

Small beat. **Fayola** *doesn't know what to do so she shifts back into comfortable territory.*

Fayola   So, I, uh, hear that you have hired Wale to play the role of James.

Gbenga   Yes, that's correct.

Fayola   He seems nice. I worked with him once, but not in a romantic film.

Gbenga   Yeah, he is a really good guy. I think you two would have great chemistry.

Fayola   Oh really?

Gbenga   But not too much, oh! Save some for others.

Fayola   Well I'm glad you haven't stopped chasing your big dreams.

Gbenga   I cannot argue with you on that one.

Fayola (*starting shit*)   Hmm . . . That may be the only thing you cannot argue with me about.

Gbenga   Really, Fayola?

Fayola   What? I did not say anything.

Gbenga   I have learned with you women, you do not need to say words to speak loudly.

Fayola   "You women" eh? . . . Oh, so I guess that eye of yours still likes to wander about.

Gbenga   Ah, Fayola, what is this, eh? I thought we decided to leave all of that in the past.

Fayola   You're right, you're right. I'm sorry I even brought it up. It's been four years and I'm over it and you are over it, so let's just, you know . . . keep it business only.

Gbenga   I agree . . . Business only.

They look into each other's eyes for a beat too long. **Gbenga** *takes* **Fayola***'s hand. He kisses the back of her hand.*

They giggle-flirt. He reluctantly lets her hand go . . . After a moment, **Ayamma** *quietly slips into the office. She keeps to the side and listens in on* **Gbenga** *and* **Fayola***'s conversation. They do not see her. You know, the classic eavesdrop situation.*

Fayola (*flirty*)   And this is business to you?

Gbenga   I don't know. Maybe . . . It's complicated.

Fayola   It always was.

Gbenga   Yes . . . Yes. It was . . .

They laugh a bit. **Ayamma** *opens the door, slams it and pretends to stumble into the room as if she's been rushing. She falls down—you know, for dramatic effect.*

Ayamma (*collecting herself—bad acting*)   Oh my goodness.

Gbenga (*helping her up*)   Eh, careful.

Ayamma   Thank you.

Gbenga   Are you okay?

Ayamma   I am. Thank you. Oh, I am so embarrassed. Look at me. My feet were moving faster than I was just to get here in time.

Gbenga   Well do not hurt yourself. I would not want that.

Ayamma *smiles a coy but alluring smile.* **Gbenga** *is immediately smitten by her charm.*

Ayamma   Thank you.

Gbenga   And you are?

Ayamma   Oh, Ayamma Okafor.

Gbenga   Ayamma, nice to meet you. I'm—

Ayamma   Gbenga Ezie. I know who you are. Such an honor to meet you. I hope I am not too late.

Gbenga   Oh no, you are not late at all.

Ayamma   I've heard it is bad luck to be the last appointment of the day.

Gbenga   Well in America, they have a saying I love: "it is good to save the best for last."

Ayamma   The best? Eh, I would not go that far.

Gbenga   Why not?

They giggle-flirt.

Fayola   Yes, why not, Gbenga?

Gbenga (*snapping out of it*)   Oh, uh, Fayola. You know how I like to give everyone a fair chance.

Ayamma   How kind of you.

Fayola (*not amused*)   Yes, how kind.

Gbenga (*to* **Ayamma**)   Do you know Fayola Ogunleye?

Ayamma   Hello! I am a huge fan of yours. I have probably seen your movie *Hungry Love* at least 100 times.

Fayola   How nice.

Ayamma   My favorite part is when you walked into the house, after you had been in prison, starving and torn down and your husband was holding that bowl of egusi and you said, "All these years without food and I've been most hungry ONLY for your love" . . . Honestly, I still cry every time I watch it.

Fayola   Thank you.

Ayamma   But my sister's personal favorite is your recent film *Corporate Office*. She is a big fan of Wale Owusu.

Fayola   Ah yes, well, he is very nice.

Ayamma   Is he? Oh, of course you would know. You are already so famous and have done so much. I really admire you.

Fayola   Thank you.

Ayamma   And it's so nice that Mr. Ezie would invite you to help him with casting who is best for the role of "Comfort." I'm sure he will benefit from your expertise and input.

Fayola *stares at* **Ayamma**. *Uncomfortable beat.*

Gbenga   Ahem, uh, Ayamma . . . Fayola is actually auditioning for the film as well.

Ayamma (*looks through script*)   Oh you are? . . . Ah, I am so silly! How could I not see—you are perfect for the role of Comfort's mother! A good looking one of course. Nothing gets in the way of good Naija skin, eh?

Fayola   For true. Not that you would know.

Ayamma   I know quite a bit, actually.

Fayola   Well . . . Ayamma—you should know that I'm actually going to be playing "Comfort."

Ayamma   Oh, has Mr. Ezie already made you an offer?

Fayola   "Mr. Ezie" does not have to offer something I already have.

Gbenga (*breaking things up*)   Eh, ladies, ladies, please. Let us just take a cool down for a moment, shall we?

Ayamma *and* **Fayola** *back away from each other but continue to hold their stares.*

Gbenga   Listen, Ayamma—don't mind her. Fayola and I just go back a number of years, but I am very happy you're here. It's exciting to see what fresh talent is out there . . . (*An idea.*) Hey. You know what might be fun? . . . Since you are both here . . . I am thinking . . . Why don't . . . uh, why don't we have you both read a scene or two . . . together? Give me a chance to see how you both fair with a scene partner . . . eh?

Tension. Finally, **Fayola** *relents and* **Ayamma** *follows.*

Ayamma   That sounds wonderful to me.

Fayola   Fine. Should be fun.

Gbenga   Great . . . Great . . . So uh, why don't we read the part where the two women: Comfort and the American wife, Rose, are meeting for the first time.

Ayamma   Wonderful.

Fayola   Great.

Gbenga   Now remember, James has been away, studying abroad in America which is where he met and fell in love with Rose. Upon his arrival back to Nigeria, he is reunited with his true love, Comfort. In this scene, Rose is in search of James—who has gone mad because he cannot decide which woman he loves more. . . Okay?

Ayamma   Okay, I'll read Comfort.   **Fayola**   Okay, I'll read Comfort.

They both look at each other for a quick beat.

Ayamma   I think it is clear that he would like for me to read for Comfort.

Fayola   Is it? You look more like a sloppy American wife to me.

Gbenga   Okay. Okay. Ladies, ladies. Please, let us not resort to improper behavior.

Ayamma (*dismissive*) Fine. I was not saying anything.	**Fayola** (*under breath*) Because you would not want me to get improper.

Gbenga   So, let's have Ayamma read for the role of Comfort—

Fayola *sucks her teeth LOUDLY.*

Gbenga   And Fayola, for the purpose of this time, you will read the role of Rose. Okay, here is a script for you.

Fayola (*snatching it*)   Thank you.

Gbenga   And for you, Ayamma—

Ayamma   Ah, it is not necessary. I have it memorized . . . Page 62, starting from the bottom section. Comfort is outside of her house drinking a cold beverage.

Ayamma *drops into her version of "Comfort" drinking a cold beverage on a hot day.* **Fayola** *rolls her eyes, but gets her game face on.*

Fayola (*as Rose—very bad American country accent that goes in and out of her natural Nigerian one*)   "Excuse me, is this the residence of James Adegbola?"

Ayamma (*as Comfort*)   "And who is asking for him?"

Fayola   "His wife from America."

Ayamma   "Eh! Who are you, witch? To speak such lies to the face of the woman he loves?"

Fayola   "I am no witch! I am his wife. From America. And I have the passport to prove it."

Ayamma   "You prove what?"

Fayola   "That I am his wife. The rightful owner of his heart."

Ayamma   "You are not the owner of anything but the devil's work!"

Fayola   "Look, is James here or no?"

Ayamma   "And if he was here, what do you need of him?"

Fayola   "Tell him, that his wife and children are here for him. I have had a vision that he has fallen mad and is walking around the streets like a wild animal, and I am here to see that he receives treatment and returns home to his family at once."

Ayamma   "If I see him, I will pass along that message. But I assure you, the only thing that James has fallen into is love. Into love with me . . . And there is nothing you and your witchcraft will do to fight it."

Gbenga   The camera zooms in on Rose's worried face.

Fayola, *slightly thrown, adjusts her face to look worried.*

Gbenga   The camera then focuses on Comfort's face of intimidation.

Ayamma *makes an intimidated face.*

Ayamma (*as Comfort*)   "Goodbye . . . Rose."

Fayola (*as Rose*)   "How did you know my name?"

Ayamma   "I am a child of God, I know everything."

Fayola *and* **Ayamma** *continue their stare down until it is broken up by* **Gbenga**.

Gbenga (*clapping*)   Wow. Wow. That was amazing. I really felt the energy and the passion. Wonderful job ladies.

Fayola   Thank you.   **Ayamma**   Thank you.

Gbenga   The story just leaped off of the page. Great work. Great, great, great.

Ayamma   What else would you like to see, Mr. Ezie? I have all of the scenes with Comfort prepared. I can perform any scene you would like to see, honestly.

Gbenga   At the present time, I have seen enough, thank you.

Fayola (*sarcasm*)   Yes, I'm sure he has seen all that you can do—

Gbenga   —But only for now. Let me think on it. I will contact you within a week's time.

Ayamma   Okay. Thank you again, Mr. Ezie. And, Fayola, I will never forget this day for the rest of my life.

Fayola   That is nice. At least one of us will remember it.

Ayamma   Well, as you just learned, memory is my strongest suit. (*To* **Gbenga**.) Have a pleasant evening.

Gbenga   You too.

Ayamma *collects her bag and exits with a coy smile.* **Gbenga** *sees her out.* **Fayola** *stands, not pleased at all, staring at* **Gbenga** *who cautiously turns around to face* **Fayola**.

Fayola   And what was that little stunt, eh?

Gbenga   Ah, Fayola, come on. I just wanted to give her a chance.

Fayola   Did you or did you not tell me, just moments before she brought her shitty little face in here, that the role of "Comfort" was mine?

Gbenga   Ah, Fayola, just calm down. It would be unfair to not let her audition.

Fayola   Let me tell you something—and you can consider this a threat if you like . . . I don't care how many pleasantries you exchange or stupid smiles you fall for, you owe me this role.

Gbenga   Fayola—

Fayola   —Eh-eh! I was going to be nice about this whole thing, but clearly, you and your wandering eyes have not learned anything over the years. (*Warning.*) You know, I am aware of many things, Gbenga.

Gbenga   Really? And what would those things be?

Fayola   What do you think your "fans" would say if they found out what you were REALLY doing in America all those years? Or how you and your brothers are REALLY getting the money to fund this project. You think I am stupid? That I cannot put three and three together? My uncle is still connected to Abacha's people. Corrupt government crooks they are, one phone call to him and your whole fraud business will go up in flames. They are catching people left and right for these 4-1-9 internet scams now.

Gbenga (*guilty*)   Internet sca—wow! You clearly do not know what you are talking about.

Fayola   Oh, so you all don't sit here all day, sending emails to people saying you are "a royal prince who has millions of dollars trapped in an overseas account and just needs five thousand dollars to get it out?"

Gbenga   Fayola—

Fayola   —I mean, honestly, the fact that people are stupid enough to believe this nonsense and wire you money, is amazing.

Gbenga   Are you finished?

Fayola   No, but you will be.

Gbenga   Wow, is this what we are doing now? Your career must really be at a low-low point for you to be blackmailing me . . . But, just know, I do not take kindly to threats. So, before you say more things you are going to regret, you should go. As I told Ayamma, I need some time to think.

Fayola   Oh, by all means, please think on it.

Fayola *walks towards the door.*

Fayola   And make sure, for once in your life, you choose with the right head.

Before she exits, she turns to **Gbenga** *one last time. They hold a look together and she exits.*

Lights shift.

Scene Six: *Adenikeh* **TV Studio**

The Adenikeh *theme song plays.* **Adenikeh** *is readying the eager audience for the entrance of her next guest. The audience cheers— they can barely contain themselves. It's a BIG show.*

Adenikeh   Thank you. Thank you so much! I know. I know! It's a BIG show! I'm sure you are all excited for today's guest, eh?

The audience cheers again.

Adenikeh   He is the hottest Nollywood movie star around. And soon, you will see him starring in the next hit film by Gbenga Ezie!

Drumroll!

Adenikeh   Ladies, please help me welcome, the beautiful, the gorgeous and the very talented WALE OWUSU!

Wale *enters to raucous applause. He smiles and waves at the audience. Perhaps blows a kiss. He is the epitome of smooth and humble. He greets* **Adenikeh** *with a hug and kiss on the cheek that she plays into as the audience continues to lose it.*

Adenikeh (*showing him off to the audience*)   Yes, he's here ladies! He's heeeeerrre!

They finally sit and the audience settles.

Wale   Wow. Thank you all so much for that warm welcome.

Adenikeh   I mean, doesn't that happen everywhere you go?

Wale   Oh no, I wish.

Adenikeh   Well, we all love you so, so much.

Wale   Thank you, Adenikeh.

Adenikeh   It's been a while since you were last on my show.

Wale   It has been some time, hasn't it? Well, I have been pretty busy over the last year—working on some really great projects.

Adenikeh   I'm sure! You are always in the most interesting and entertaining films and many of us have marveled at your work over the years, but you are always playing a liar! A stealer! A cheater!. . . So, I have to ask, are you anything like some of those characters?

"Ooohs" are heard from the audience.

Wale (*laughs*)   Oh, well I have had the good fortune of playing all sorts of roles and, yes, most of them are less than honorable men, but I don't think I am anything like them.

Adenikeh   But that is what an   **Wale**   Of course.
actor dreams of, yes?

Adenikeh   Getting to play a variety of roles?

Wale   We all want to be challenged by the work.

Adenikeh   Yes, your last film *Here Comes the Alien Invasion, Oh*! was a blockbuster—with many critics calling it the Nollywood version of *Star Wars*.

Wale   Yes, I was humbled at the comparison. I mean, we all grew up watching all of those Hollywood alien movies.

Adenikeh   You mention Hollywood—have you ever set your sights on America?

Wale   Oh I would love to work there. Mixing with the likes of Denzel Washington or Morgan Freeman. Maybe even win an Oscar. Can you imagine? But for now, I think I'll be getting a taste of American life in Gbenga Ezie's new film.

Adenikeh   Yes, *The Comfort Zone*! We are all extremely excited for the release! Have you all started shooting yet?

Wale   No, Gbenga is still holding auditions for my love interest.

Adenikeh   Eh-eh? Love interest?!

Wale   In the film.

Adenikeh   Ah, I see. And speaking of love, that is something you have been very private about recently. We all remember your last relationship to the sultry, sexy singer, Angela Chukwu. It was quite public. I can't imagine having reporters and paparazzi everywhere you go. That must have been a lot to deal with.

Wale   Yes, it was. And a relationship can only last so long under that kind of spotlight—that constant media scrutiny. I learned a lot about the value of privacy. Certainly put "fame" into perspective.

Adenikeh   I understand. But I hope you have not given up on love, have you? I'm sure many of my viewers would like me to inquire as to whether you are connected to any particular woman right now?

The women in the audience "oooh."

Wale (*smiling his winning smile*)   No, no, I am not. I am still in search for the one.

Adenikeh   Well I am sure I have plenty of volunteers to be "your one" in my audience today, eh?

The audience, mainly the women, clap and scream with spirited delight.

Adenikeh   ESPECIALLY after being named—

She pulls out a magazine.

Adenikeh   "Nigeria's Sexiest Man Born." Look at you!

The audience of women clap and scream a bit louder at the sight of **Wale***'s magazine cover.*

Wale (*laughs; trying to speak over the chaos of screams and clapping*)   Oh goodness. Thank you.

Adenikeh (*to camera*)   Okay, ladies, grab some cold water, yeah—and please keep your television sets on this program. We will be back with more of Wale Owusu on *Adenikeh*!

The Adenikeh *theme song plays out with audience applause.*

Scene Seven: Okafor Travel Agency Office

Ayamma *is on the phone. After a moment,* **Dede** *enters.*

Ayamma   . . . So we'll finish this up for you and send your tickets right away . . . You're welcome. Have a good day.

Ayamma *hangs up the phone—sullen and sad.*

Dede   Who was that on the phone?

Ayamma   Just a customer . . . And not Gbenga offering me the role of Comfort.

Ayamma *sighs deeply and continues to sulk.*

Dede (*over it*)   Ayamma . . . This "Queen of Sorrow" act is too much. It's just one movie. There will be other opportunities.

Ayamma   How do you know that?

Dede   As sure as I have fallen down and gotten back up again with no problems . . . You see, as good as I am at everything, that's why I never did the acting. It makes you people go crazy.

Ayamma   That is not true.

Dede   Its not? Then how come you are beating up that computer so? Is the computer named Fayola?

Ayamma   I told you to never say her name again.

Dede (*sucks teeth*)   Look, you'll feel better soon. I'm sure the curse I put on her will start taking its effect momentarily.

Ayamma   Dede, your curses never work.

Dede   This will be the one that kicks in, just wait.

The phone rings.

Dede   I got it. I got it. (*Answers.*) Hello. Thank you for calling Okafor Travels. This is Dede. How may I help you? (*Listens.*) Eh, Mary! How are you? (*Listens.*) What? It is happening now? Oh my goodness. Okay, okay. I'm coming over.

Dede *hangs up and rushes to grab her purse and some sort of snack.*

Ayamma   Where are you going?

Dede   Mary's salon! Stefano is forcing Marlena to choose! I can't miss it!

Ayamma   Dede—

Dede (*leaving*)   I'm coming. I'm coming.

Dede *exits.* **Ayamma** *sits annoyed shaking her head. The phone rings again and* **Ayamma** *answers it angrily.*

Ayamma   This is Okafor Travels. What would you like? (*Listens.*) Okay, miss. Slow down. You want what? . . . A flight to where? . . . I'm sorry, please repeat that. Your connection is faulty.

The front door chimes as it opens and **Gbenga** *and* **Wale Owusu** *enter.*

Gbenga   Let's just copy these new pages of the script here so we don't have to go all the way back to my office.

Wale   Sounds good.

Ayamma (*struggling to hear*)   What? I'm sorry. SPEAK LOUDER PLEASE. I CANNOT HEAR YOU WELL . . . You say what?

Gbenga   Excuse me . . .

Gbenga *and* **Wale** *stare at* **Ayamma** *struggling on the phone.* **Ayamma** *eventually turns to them.*

Ayamma (*to* **Gbenga** *and* **Wale**)   I will be with you in moment. (*Double take; into phone.*) Umm, lady, please call back when you have a better connection. Bye!

Ayamma *hangs up the phone quickly and nearly leaps to her feet smiling and trying to adjust herself.*

Ayamma   Mr. Ezie.

Gbenga   Ayamma. What a pleasant surprise.

Ayamma   It is indeed. How are you?

Gbenga   Oh, fine, fine. And you?

Ayamma (*smiles awkwardly*)   Oh, you know . . . just . . .

Gbenga   I did not know you worked here.

Ayamma   Yes, yes. This is my parents' business. They travel a lot, so my sister and I do most of the work around here.

Gbenga   Well, the next time I am booking a trip somewhere, I know who to come to. I trust you will give me a good price.

Ayamma   Oh sure. Of course.

Gbenga   Fine, fine.

Small beat. It's kind of awkward.

Ayamma (*to* **Wale**)   Uh . . . Hello.

Gbenga   Ah! My manners have flown out of the window. Yes, Wale, this is Ayamma.

Wale   Yes, I've gathered that. I'm—

Ayamma   Wale Owusu! I know who you are. I am a HUGE fan.

Wale *sends a warm, genuine smile* **Ayamma***'s way. She becomes transfixed and smitten all at once (his usual effect).*

Wale   Oh, thank you. That is very nice of you to say.

Ayamma   It is true. My sister and I can watch your movies over and over again.

Wale   Thank you.

Ayamma   Seriously. Just over and over and over—

Wale   Thank you. Thank you. I understand.

Ayamma   Sorry.

Wale   It is okay—

Ayamma   —I am a bit nervous. It is not everyday that big movie stars like you come walking into our office.

Wale   Well, it is not everyday that I meet someone who watches my movies over . . . and over . . . and over again.

Wale *and* **Ayamma** *laugh. Her nerves subside a bit.* **Wale** *is clearly curious about* **Ayamma**. **Gbenga** *notices their chemistry.*

Wale   So uh, how do you two know each other?

Gbenga   Ayamma came in to audition for *The Comfort Zone* last week.

Wale   Oh, you are an actress?

Ayamma   Oh, just aspiring. I do not have a resume nearly as impressive as yours.

Wale   Ah, come now. If there is anything I know is that talent is subjective. But if you have the spirit and the passion—eventually the work will come.

Ayamma (*smiles*)   I will heed your advice. Thank you.

Wale   You are most welcome.

They smile at each other some more. **Ayamma** *eventually snaps out of it.*

Ayamma   So, is there something I can help you two with?

Gbenga   Ah yes, I was wondering if you all have a xerox machine that I may use? I am willing to pay whatever your rates are.

Ayamma   Oh, no please. Its "on the house." How many papers do you need copied?

Gbenga (*handing her the papers*)   Just these three.

Ayamma   Okay. Please, have a seat.

Ayamma *walks over to the xerox machine and begins to make the copies as* **Gbenga** *and* **Wale** *sit.*

Gbenga   You know, Ayamma . . . It's funny that I am running into you like this. I was actually going to call you this evening.

Ayamma (*not facing him*)   Oh?

Gbenga   Yes, I wanted to talk to you about your audition.

Ayamma   Oh?

Gbenga   I thought you gave a really strong interpretation to the role of "Comfort." And I was very impressed that you had all of those lines committed to memory.

Wale   That is impressive.

Ayamma   Thank you.

Gbenga   And I know it was not easy to be reading that scene alongside Fayola. She is very tough as you see.

Ayamma   I noticed.

Gbenga   Anyway, I just wanted to thank you for coming in. It was very nice meeting you and I will certainly keep you in mind for future projects.

Ayamma (*upset but tries to keep herself composed*)   Okay.

Small beat. **Wale** *silently urges* **Gbenga** *ala "Come on, man!"*

Gbenga   But . . . In the mean time . . . Are you free to come in for a call back next week?

Ayamma (*zooms around to look at him*)   A what?

Gbenga   Call back. I would like to see you read a few scenes with Wale . . . What we in the industry call a "chemistry read."

Ayamma *is stunned silent.*

Gbenga   Unless you are having reservations—

Ayamma   No, no! I would love to come in for a back call.

Gbenga   Call back—

Ayamma   —Call back.

Ayamma *walks back over to* **Gbenga** *and* **Wale** *and hands him his copies.*

Gbenga   Great. Can you come down to the studio offices on Wednesday at 4 p.m.?

Ayamma   Yes. Of course.

Gbenga   Wonderful. I am looking forward to it.

Gbenga *extends his hand and shakes* **Ayamma***'s hand.*

Ayamma   Me too.

Wale   Me three.

Wale *extends his hand.* **Ayamma** *and* **Wale***'s eyes remained locked on each other, smiling. Chemistry.*

Scene Eight: Ezie's Nollywood Dreams Studios

Dede *sits in a chair, checking herself out in the mirror. She fixes her hair, re-applies her lipstick, adjusts herself until she is satisfied with how her chest looks in her dress.* **Ayamma** *enters and immediately starts to pace nervously while silently reviewing her lines.*

Dede   Did the taxi driver give you a good price?

Ayamma   Yes.

Dede   Good. Because I'm too nervous to be arguing about money today . . . (*Slight whisper.*) So, will he be coming in through that door or is there some secret passage at the back of the office?

Ayamma   I don't know. He will probably come in through the front here.

Dede   Okay.

Dede *sits impatiently for a beat. She tries to leave* **Ayamma** *alone, but can't help herself.*

Dede   Now will I be allowed to talk to him or is he going to just be rushed into a private room or something?

Ayamma   Dede, please. I am trying to concentrate on this.

Dede   I'm sorry. So sorry. Go ahead.

Dede *sits quietly for a moment. She then whips out her mirror and "practises" how she will smile and greet* **Wale** *when he arrives. Perhaps she says "Hello Wale" a few times.* **Ayamma** *becomes distracted by* **Dede***'s actions.*

Ayamma   Come on, Dede.

Dede   What? I need to know what I will look like when I meet him.

Ayamma   He is not coming here for you! This is serious movie business! You are lucky I let you come here with me.

Dede   No, YOU are lucky that I allowed myself to come here.

Ayamma   Dede—

Dede   What? I'm the one who should still be furious with you.

Ayamma   With me? For what?

Dede   For not calling me when Wale was in our office that day! I was just down the road at Mary's Salon. And you did not think to call me? How hard is it for you to pick up the phone and say "Hey sista, you know your future husband Wale Owusu? Well, he is standing right here in front of me. I will club him over the head, tie him up, keep him here until you can come with a pastor in tow so when he wakes up, you will be married and begin your life with him." I mean honestly!

Ayamma   Dede, there is no time for your antics today. If you ruin my chance to get in this movie, I will never forgive you. And so help me God that—

Gbenga *and* **Wale** *enter laughing and carrying on.* **Ayamma** *immediately drops the rage and pulls herself together.* **Dede** *is shocked at the sight of* **Wale** *and immediately hides.*

Gbenga   Ayamma! Good to see you! Here ON time and not African time.

They all laugh a bit.

Ayamma   I am a very punctual person.

Gbenga   I see that. Good to know . . . Eh, Wale, you remember Ayamma.

Wale   Yes. It is good to see you again. You look very nice today.

Ayamma   Oh, I just purchased this dress at the shopping center.

Wale   Well, I hope you got the last one because surely no other woman will fit it as lovely as you.

Ayamma (*flattered*)   Thank you, Wale.

Dede *clears her throat inappropriately loud. She stands and saunters over to stand next to* **Ayamma**.

Gbenga   Oh, and who do we have we here?

Ayamma   Mr. Ezie, this is my sister Dede.

Gbenga (*shaking her hand*)   Nice to meet you.

Dede   And you as well.

Gbenga   You should be very proud of your sister here. She has been doing some excellent work in this audition process.

Dede   Oh, me, I'm always very proud of her.

Ayamma   Umm and, Dede, this is Wale Owusu.

Wale   Well, it is clear that good looks are quite strong in your family.

Wale *takes* **Dede**'s *hand and kisses it.* **Dede** *smiles and lets out a very squeaky laugh . . . And that's pretty much all she can do. She is struck dumb by* **Wale**'s *good looks and charm.*

Wale   It is a pleasure to meet you. You know, in my father's family, Dede is a common name. Are one of your parents from Ghana as well?

Dede *smiles and laughs.*

Ayamma   Uh, our mother went to University in Accra. She fell in love with the names of her school mates so she named us in kind.

Wale   Ah, I see. Well, I have always loved that name . . . Dede. Are you an actress as well?

Dede *smiles and laughs.*

Ayamma   No, actually, this is the sister I was telling you about— who works with me as an agent at Okafor Travels.

Gbenga   Ah yes, well, I have always been an advocator of keeping business in the family.

Wale   I agree. And it certainly must be nice to work alongside your sister everyday. I can tell you two are quite close. Yes?

Ayamma   Yes, we see each other all the time. So it is nice when we get to go places and do things on our own. Speaking of which, you should go now, Dede. I do not want you to be late for that thing you were telling me about.

Dede (*smiles . . . then as she rehearsed it*)   Hello, Wale. My name is Dede.

Wale *smiles back in kind.*

Ayamma   Yes, sista, we have already established that . . . Listen, I think it is time for you to go. I do not want to hold up these busy men any further.

Ayamma *pushes* **Dede** *to the door and* **Dede** *remains transfixed on* **Wale***.*

Gbenga (*checks watch*)   Uh, actually, do you all mind if I step out for a moment. I have an important package to pick up at Western Union. I will only be a short while, do you mind, Ayamma?

Ayamma   No, that is fine. I understand.

Gbenga   I will be back in no time. And you know, you two can chat a bit more. Get to know each other.

Wale   I would love that.

Gbenga   Great. Okay. (*To* **Dede**.) Eh, Dede . . . Can I drop you somewhere close to your destination?

Ayamma (*to* **Gbenga**)   Uh, if you are going by downtown then yes, we would most appreciate that.

Gbenga   Not a problem. (*As if talking to a child.*) Come, Dede. My driver is just this way.

Ayamma *pushes* **Dede** *towards the door with* **Gbenga** *kindly assisting her. With one final push,* **Dede** *and* **Gbenga** *exit.*

Ayamma   Sorry about that. As I mentioned, she really, really loves your work.

Wale   That is fine. I am more than happy to talk to a fan. Although, I do not know how much talking she does.

Ayamma   Trust me. That is only time I have ever seen her quiet.

Wale   I see.

They laugh a bit. Beat.

Wale   Would you like some water?

Ayamma   Sure.

Wale *pours a glass of water from the cooler for* **Ayamma**. *He pours himself a glass as well.*

Ayamma   Ugh, you have to forgive me. I am a bit nervous about this back call.

Wale   Callback.

Ayamma   Callback.

Wale   It is fine. Just some silly industry talk. You will learn it all in time.

Ayamma   Okay

Wale *hands* **Ayamma** *the glass of water.*

Wale   They say it is bad luck to toast with water, but let's forget the superstition for now.

Ayamma   What are we toasting to?

Wale   To us: that you may release any nerves you are feeling and that we have an amazing audition today.

Ayamma   I will toast to that . . . Although you are not really auditioning.

Wale   Oh, I am. To be your love.

Ayamma   Pardon?

Wale   In the movie.

Ayamma   Oh, right. Of course.

They clink cups and drink.

Ayamma   Ooh, and it is cold. Even better.

Wale   Only the best at Nollywood Dreams Studios.

Ayamma   I see that.

Wale (*gesturing for her to sit*)   Please.

Beat.

Ayamma   So . . . you were born in Ghana?

Wale   Yes, but I grew up here.

Ayamma   Right, because your mother is Nigerian. I know practically everything about you.

Wale   Oh?

Ayamma   Well, my sister reads all of the gossip magazines. And, well, they write about you a lot.

Wale   Ah, I see. Though you can't always believe everything you read.

Ayamma   So . . . It's not true that you and Angela Chukwu broke up?

Wale   Ah, well. . that is true.

Ayamma   I'm sorry to hear that.

Wale   Don't be. I think we both knew it was over for quite some time. She enjoyed all the attention and the fame.

Ayamma   Come now, and you don't?

Wale   Don't get me wrong: fame has its perks. But, me, I'm a lowkey kind of guy. I'm fine with going to the beach, making some dinner or just reading a book.

Ayamma   I know. I much prefer a book myself.

Wale   Have you heard of this new one: *Chicken Soup for the Soul?* Americans are going crazy over it.

Ayamma   It is about food?

Wale   Sort of. Food for your mind.

Ayamma   You sound like my father. He is always picking up some quote or custom everywhere he goes.

Wale   Ah yes. You said your parents travel a lot together?

Ayamma   Yes, mostly for business. Meeting new clients and investors. It is not very romantic.

Wale   Mmm, I think doing anything with the person you love can be romantic.

Ayamma *makes a "is he for real" face.*

Ayamma   Okay, Wale. I have to ask. Are you always like this?

Wale   Like what?

Ayamma   All smooth, smooth, like this? Always saying and doing the right things?

Wale (*smiling that smile only he can do*)   What do you mean?

Ayamma   That! Are you putting on a show for me or is this really how you are?

Wale   I assure you. This is just who I am.

Ayamma   Okay.

Wale   I can ease back a bit if you want.

Ayamma   No, no. I am fine.

Wale   So I should remain as I am?

Ayamma   I do not want you to change anything or do anything. You are fine . . . More than fine.

Wale (*curiously flirty*)   More than fine?

Ayamma   Wale, please. You know that every woman from the top to the very bottom of Nigeria thinks that you are handsome. I appreciate the humble act, but . . . come on.

Wale   No, you're right. It is certainly something that I am quite flattered by. But in this moment, I am most interested to know what you think of me.

Ayamma   Why?

Wale   Because I think . . . you are truly something, Ayamma Okafor.

Ayamma   What makes you say so?

Wale   Everything.

Ayamma   Everything of what?

Wale   Everything that men from the top to the very bottom of Nigeria are searching for.

Ayamma   Oh . . . uh, thank you.

Wale   You are most welcome.

Small beat. **Ayamma** *is flustered.* **Wale** *drinks his water.*

Ayamma   Well, how about we get to the matter at hand, eh? Can I ask you some questions about this scene?

Wale   Sure.

Ayamma   Well, James is clearly saying all of the right things to Comfort, but it not clear where his heart truly lies. What is your opinion? Is he in love with Comfort or does he want to have one last thrill before he goes back to his wife and family in America?

Wale   Hmmm . . . I guess it depends on how you want to look at it. How are you so sure that James is not just saying what is on his heart? Comfort is his soulmate. His one true love. Its only that he did not know he would ever see her again.

Ayamma   But he is married. He has moved on.

Wale   Yes, he has moved on, but his heart has not.

Ayamma   Oh come on.

Wale   What?

Ayamma   Ugh, you men. You're all the same. Even in a script! You want to mix, bake, have your cake, put it in the fridge, never touch it for a long while and then expect it to be sitting there when YOU are ready to eat it. It's so frustrating.

Wale   That's good.

Ayamma   Good?

Wale   Yes, draw from that frustration. This is exactly what Comfort is feeling in this moment.

Ayamma (*trying to follow*)   Okay . . .

Wale   That is the secret: Connect the emotion to something you have felt in real life and it will shine on camera.

Ayamma   Really?

Wale   Yes, really. You are going to be amazing.

Wale *smiles at* **Ayamma** *and she blushes again. Their sweet moment is broken up as* **Gbenga** *enters with* **Fayola** *following close behind him.*

Gbenga   I am back. And look at who I ran into.

Wale   Fayola. Good to see you again.

Wale *and* **Fayola** *exchange a kiss on the cheek.* **Ayamma** *strains a smile.*

Fayola   Wale! It has been so long. How have you been?

Wale   Very well, I cannot complain. And you?

Fayola   Fabulous, as usual.

Gbenga   And, Fayola, you remember Ayamma.

Fayola   Yes. There you are.

Ayamma   Good to see you again, Fayola.

Gbenga   Please pardon my scheduling failures. I thought I could get to Western Union and back before the times could be crossed.

Ayamma   That is okay.

Wale   Yes . . . Ayamma and I used the time quite wisely.

Fayola   Did you now?

Wale   I always like getting to know my scene partner. Brings me back to my University days.

Gbenga   Ah yes. The good old days of improv and silly exercises.

They all laugh a bit.

Fayola   You guys, please. Don't make Ayamma feel bad. Clearly, she could not afford a collegiate education.

Ayamma   Actually I have a degree in business finance.

Fayola   Oh, you do? Wonderful. I will be sure to keep you in mind when I am looking for a new accountant.

Ayamma   If I am not already busy . . . With filming and such.

Fayola   Ha! Did you get a degree in comedy as well?

Gbenga   Okay well, great. We are all acquainted. Ayamma, since you're first, why don't we head back to one of the rehearsal studios.

Fayola   Oh! You don't want to have us read with each other again Gbenga? I thought that was "your thing."

Gbenga   I just want everyone to be comfortable.

Fayola   I'm comfortable. Wale, are you fine?

Wale   Uhhh—

Fayola   —And you, Ayamma? You were so impressive the last time, I just assume you have no fear in doing it again.

Ayamma   I don't.

Fayola   Good. Then I say, not to be a dictator, but why don't we have a friendly reading session right here. You're not expecting any other appointments, are you, Gbenga?

Gbenga (*does not like* **Fayola**'s *little game*)   No, I am not.

Fayola   Ah, so it IS down to the two of us. Interesting.

Gbenga   I did not say that.

Fayola   Now, which scene would you like us to start with first?

Wale   Is this okay with you, Ayamma?

Ayamma   Of course.

Gbenga   But it is not okay with me. So, if you will excuse us—

Ayamma   No, Mr. Ezie. I am perfectly fine.

Fayola   You see, "Mr. Ezie" . . . She is fine.

Gbenga   Are you sure?

Ayamma   Yes.

Fayola   Then it is settled.

Ayamma   Great. Why don't you go first, Fayola.

Fayola   Oh, for you to take notes?

Ayamma   No, for you to get off of my way.

Fayola *and* **Ayamma** *share an evil smile at each other.*

Fayola   Fine . . . Wale are you ready?

Wale *is confused by the tension between* **Fayola** *and* **Ayamma**.

Wale   Uh, yeah, sure.

Gbenga (*sighs*)   Okay, let's start from the top of page 81.

Fayola   Lovely.

Gbenga   Alright, whenever you two are ready, you can begin.

Gbenga *takes a seat, seemingly exhausted from the energy in the room.* **Fayola** *and* **Wale** *review their scripts for a moment.* **Fayola** *faces away from* **Wale***, turns coyly over her shoulder and nods to him that she is ready.*

Wale (*as James*)   "Comfort, is that you?"

Fayola (*as Comfort*)   "I am here. Do you not see me standing here, plain as the day."

Wale   "I came as soon as I received your message. What is troubling you?"

Fayola   "So many things. I do not even know where to begin."

Wale   "Then start at the top of the list."

Fayola   "Okay, first on the list . . . My heart."

Wale   "What has happened to it? Have you fallen ill?"

Fayola   "No I have fallen in love. Again. With you."

Wale   "And what is wrong with that?"

Fayola   "What is wrong is that you have taken my heart and broken it into a million pieces."

Wale   "What are you talking about? What have I done to cause you this pain?"

Fayola   "Oh, I do not know. Maybe it has something to do with your wife . . . Or your children."

Gbenga (*reading stage directions*)   Close up on James' face as he takes this news in. How did she find out?

Wale *as "James" acts taking in the news.*

Fayola   "Yes, I know . . . All about everything. She came to visit me and told me all about how you have taken a wife in America and had children with her."

Wale   "Yes. It is true. But so are my feelings for you."

Fayola   "How can you say that to me? How can you look me in my pained face and say that to me. Have you no shame?"

Wale   "I HAVE PLENTY OF SHAME!"

Fayola   "YES, I SEE THAT!"

Gbenga   AND HOLD! Okay, let's hold here. Thank you very much, Fayola, that was wonderful.

Fayola   I was just getting warmed up.

Gbenga   Yes . . . Thank you. I really felt your "heat." But I would like to see what Ayamma does with the rest of the scene.

Fayola   Sure.

Gbenga   Okay, so, Ayamma, let's just pick up from where we left off. Is that fine?

Ayamma   Of course.

Ayamma *and* **Fayola** *cross each other.*

Fayola (*to* **Ayamma**—*loaded*)   Break a leg.

Ayamma *is not sure what that means, but shakes it off.* **Wale** *smiles at her with encouragement.*

Wale   Just let me know when you are ready.

Ayamma   I am ready.

Wale (*as James*)   "So tell me, Comfort. What do you want me to say?"

Ayamma (*as Comfort*)   "I want you to tell me the truth."

Wale   "I always tell you the truth! . . . Except for that one small thing about my wife and children."

Ayamma   "I want you to tell me, was any of it real?"

Wale   "Was what real?"

Ayamma   "How we would stay up all night talking about nothing? Or the way you look at me when I fix you a plate of stew.

Or the way you sing me all the songs we made up when we were children? Was any of that real, James? I need to know. My heart needs to know."

Wale   "Comfort, everything I do and say to you is real. But, me, I'm caught between a rock and a very hard surface."

Ayamma   "Well then I will make it easy for you. I am tired of being your rock. (*more*)

I deserve more than your half love. I cannot give you everything if you cannot give me the same."

Gbenga   Comfort begins to walk away.

Wale   "COMFORT, WAIT!"

Ayamma   "NO!. . . No, James . . . I cannot be your Comfort zone . . . anymore."

Gbenga   Close up on Comfort as she turns away from James and cries.

Ayamma *as "Comfort" turns away and cries—on cue.*

Gbenga (*claps*)   And let's hold here. Wow. Wonderful work, Ayamma. Absolutely wonderful.

Ayamma   Thank you.

Gbenga   And, Wale, great job. As always.

Wale (*humble*)   Oh, thanks.

Gbenga   Wow. You know. I have a lot to think on. Ayamma, thank you so much again for coming. It has truly been a pleasure to watch you work. You are quite a talent.

Ayamma   Oh, Mr. Ezie. This has been amazing. I have learned so much in this process.

Gbenga   I'm glad to hear it. I will be in touch by tomorrow morning, okay?

Ayamma   Okay. Looking forward to hearing from you. . . . Bye, Fayola.

Fayola   Mmm hmm.

Ayamma (*fondly*)   And thank you, Wale. For everything as well.

Wale   Just a moment—may I walk you home?

Ayamma   Uh, if you want to.

Wale   I would love to. (*Opens the door for her.*) After you . . .

Ayamma   Thank you . . .

Wale *and* **Ayamma** *exit.*

Fayola (*breaking the silence*)   So, that was cute . . . You know she is going to be heartbroken when you tell her she did not get the part.

Gbenga   Who has said I have made up my mind?

Fayola   Still playing with fire?

Gbenga   No, I am just not playing with you, Fayola. I told you, I don't take kindly to threats.

Fayola   Then imagine how you will take to prison.

Gbenga   You know, Fayola. I could never keep up with your moods. They change faster than the Harmattan winds!

Fayola   Oh please. Nothing about me has ever changed.

Gbenga   Oh, trust me. I see that.

Fayola   And clearly you are still into childish behavior—

Gbenga   And here it is—

Fayola   —Yes, here it is—

Gbenga   —I think all you like to do is yell and fight, you know that?—

Fayola   —Yelling and fighting? How about lying and cheating, eh?—

Gbenga   Fayola, I was always, ALWAYS, honest with you. I told you about everything—

Fayola   —Of course you did! After I confronted you. What do you not understand, Gbenga? I sacrificed EVERYTHING for you and / you just—

Gbenga   —For me? / Ha!

Fayola   —Excuse me? Yes, you! You are the one who begged me to come and be with you in New York! "It will all be fine, Fayola. No one has to know that I did not get into NYU. I will just re-apply and it will all be fine-fine."

Gbenga   But I did not force you! You are the one who said you wanted a "fresh start."

Fayola   Oh, so a "fresh start" is sitting in a cold apartment, in a scary city, miles away from my family, waiting for you to come home at night? Lying to everyone that you were doing so well in film school when you were just a janitor? Or are you talking about the "fresh start" you were trying to have with that white girl?

Gbenga   AND WHAT CHOICE DID I HAVE?!

They didn't make anything easy for us over there! All I was trying to do was make movies. Have a better life! But I spent most of my time scared that immigration was going to throw me in jail. All for what?

Because I wanted to make art?! . . . Marrying her was my only choice. The only way I knew I would be able to stay and make a good life. It was all just for the papers! And as soon as everything cleared, I was going to move you to Hollywood and make you a star. How come you cannot understand that I was only with her for our sake?!

Fayola   Do you hear your mouth right now? And how did that plan work out for you? Hmm? That white girl dropped you faster than you could turn your head . . . Just like every other African man—you were sick with "American Fever." Don't you understand, to them, you are nothing but another Black man? A nigga with an accent . . . You think I didn't hear about how she turned you over to immigration? Hmmm? And how they sent you back home on a plane, barefoot . . . with nothing . . .

Gbenga   That's what you think happened, eh?

Fayola   I don't think—I know.

Gbenga   And who are your sources? How many people have they shared this with?

Fayola   Look at you. Still ONLY concerned about yourself. Only concerned about what people are saying about you, you, you!

Gbenga   Fayola—

Fayola   —Before I left Nigeria, I had it all: a wonderful career, family and friends. I was happy. I didn't need American success—I had my own—right here. And I left it all behind because I believed in you and your dreams . . . But you never thought about me . . . You never cared about me or what I was going through. Just took off to Los Angeles with that white girl trying to "sell your script." . . . And you didn't call, come back or apologize to me. Not even once . . . Not even now . . .

And after all these years, here I am, trying to piece together my career again. Asking you of all people, to give me the chance to reclaim what I have lost trying to help YOU succeed . . . Do you know what this is like for me?

Gbenga   I'm sorry.

Fayola   You always said you wanted to "make me the star." Here is your chance.

Fayola *collects her things and begins to walk out.* **Gbenga** *stops her.*

Gbenga   I am slated to get a large wire of money tomorrow. We will start filming in two weeks. I will have my sister get in touch for your measurements. She is the costume designer for the film.

Fayola   Great. It will be nice to catch up with Ade again.

Gbenga   Yes.

Fayola   . . . Thank you.

Fayola *leaves.* **Gbenga** *sits. Lights shift*

Scene Nine: Okafor Travel Agency

Dede *is on the couch doing her usual: snacking and watching television. The phone rings and she turns down the TV.* **Ayamma** *enters holding grocery bags. She sulks as she sets the bags on a desk and starts taking things out.*

Dede (*answering*)   Thank you for calling Okafor Travels. This is Dede, how may I help you? (*Listens.*) Mommy, how are you? (*To* **Ayamma**.) It's Mommy and Daddy. (*Back into phone.*) No we are fine . . . "You know who" is still "depression" or whatever, but other than that things are fine . . . When will you be back? (*Listens.*) Oh, okay. That is great . . . (*More.*) Yes, we are getting everything done. We are sorting out all of the files right now actually . . . Yes, me too! . . . You are disturbing me . . . Disturbing both of us . . . Okay . . . Okay . . . Alright, talk to you soon . . . Love you too. Bye bye. (*To* **Ayamma**.) Mommy says hi.

Ayamma   Thanks for letting me talk to her.

Dede   She did not ask for you, Madame Sadness.

Ayamma   Whatever.

Dede (*eventually*)   Were you able to get more tea.

Ayamma   Yes.

Dede   And ginger cookies?

Ayamma   Yes.

Dede   Thanks.

Small beat.

Dede   It's been a bit slow today. And, uh . . . You did not get any calls . . . In case you were going to ask.

Ayamma   It has been four days. At this point, I'm not expecting any calls.

Dede   . . . You know, Ayamma, I have been watching a lot of Adenikeh lately and she always says we should stay positive and have forward thinking . . . Perhaps you will have an "eh heh" moment.

Ayamma   What?

Dede   An "eh heh" moment. You know, when you understand why things happened the way that they did.

Ayamma   Whatever . . . Adenikeh does not know what the hell she is talking about.

Dede   Eh-eh! Do not talk about Adenikeh like this. She is like a television mother to me.

Ayamma (*sarcasm*)   Sorry.

Ayamma *puts on a teapot of water and sets a cup on the counter. Then slams things around.*

Dede *shakes her head and embraces her sister.* **Ayamma** *allows it and hugs her back.*

Dede   It is going to be okay "Yamma." You will be just fine— trust me. (*More.*) (*Small beat. Doesn't want to admit this, but . . .*) You know, I have to admit, you are pretty good at this acting thing. I was very impressed when we were rehearsing for your callback.

Ayamma   Seriously?

Dede   Yes . . . I mean, obviously not as good as the raw talent I clearly have, but you know, you're not so bad after all.

Ayamma   Thank you. That means a lot coming from you. But it's still sad though.

Dede   I know . . . All of that money gone . . .

Ayamma *rolls her eyes and releases the hug.*

Ayamma (*sarcasm*)   Really, Dede? Is that all you are thinking about?

Dede (*sucks teeth*)   But, don't worry, I can feel in my spirit that the curse I put on Fayola is going to take force soon.

Ayamma   Dede please.

Dede   What? It's true. (*Looks at watch.*) (*More.*) Eh, where is Mary? She said was going to bring me some new movie videos that she thought I would like.

The door chimes. It's **Wale**—*standing there smiling with his beautiful face.*

Pause.

Dede   You are not Mary.

Wale   Well not today, no I am not.

Dede *smiles and laughs.*

Wale   Dede! It is good to see you again. You are looking lovely as ever.

Dede *smiles and laughs.*

Ayamma *walks over to the door.*

Ayamma (*surprised*)   Wale? What are you doing here?

Wale   Ayamma—I was hoping that you would be working today.

Dede *remains transfixed on* **Wale** *as he steps in.*

Ayamma   Well, you have to excuse us. The office has been neglected a bit. We were just about to straighten things up.

Wale   Sorry. I did not mean to just barrel in like so, I just wanted to talk to you.

Ayamma   Oh?

Wale   . . . How are you?

Ayamma   I have had better days, but I am okay.

Ayamma *and* **Wale** *both notice* **Dede** *smiling.*

Ayamma   Dede, do you mind stepping into the back room for some moments?

Dede   Sure.

Wale   Good to see you, Dede.

Dede *smiles and laughs and nods and faintly says "Wale".*

Dede *exits—smiling at* **Wale***.*

Ayamma   So . . . Are you interested in booking a trip?

Wale   No . . . I just . . . I wanted to see you again.

Ayamma   Oh . . . For what?

Wale   Just because.

Ayamma   Well I'm surprised you have the time with your busy schedule. Haven't you already started filming?

Wale   We start shooting next week.

Ayamma   That's great. Congratulations. I'm sure you all are going to have a wonderful time.

Wale   Ayamma . . .

Ayamma   Would you like some tea?

Wale   Please.

Ayamma *checks on the water for the tea. She fetches another cup from the cabinet and sets it on the counter next to hers.*

Wale   Ayamma, have I done something to upset you?

Ayamma   What makes you say that?

Wale   Well I haven't heard from you in a while.

Ayamma   I've been busy.

Wale   Okay . . . I was just hoping to see you again soon. I really enjoyed our walk home that night after your audition.

Ayamma   I did too.

Wale   So why the cold shoulders then?

Ayamma   It's just . . . Seeing you reminds me that I am not going to be in the movie and I know that I was born to play that part.

Wale   Yeah? And how do you know that?

Ayamma   Because I feel it. Felt it . . . Look, you don't understand, Wale . . . I grew up, went to school and live in the same town where I work for my parents at this travel agency and I've never even left Lagos! I don't come from wealth and access like you or Fayola. So that open call was my shot—my one chance to get out there and see if maybe I can make my dreams come true . . . To be like the women in all of those Hollywood films I spent my life watching . . . So, to not get the role . . . It just makes me sad . . . It might seem silly to you, but that's how I feel.

Wale   I understand. And I'm sorry too. But what if all of this happened for another reason? Another purpose?

Ayamma   Wale, please. I know you like sharing things from those "life lesson" books, but—

Wale   Yes and one thing I have come to understand is that you may never know why you meet certain people or are called to certain places. Perhaps there is a bigger, sometimes better plan in store for you. So yes, you did not get this part, but there will be others. Trust me.

Ayamma   Spoken by the big movie star.

Wale   Is that all I am to you? . . . I thought maybe I was your friend as well.

Ayamma   You can be my friend if you want.

Wale   Yes I very much would . . . I'd also like to be more than your friend. . . After a time of course . . . Is that okay too?

Beat.

Dede (*O.S.*)   YES! THAT IS PERFECTLY FINE! AND IF SHE DOESN'T WANT TO BE YOUR FRIEND, I WILL! I WILL BE YOUR ANYTHING!

Ayamma *and* **Wale** *laugh.*

Ayamma   What she said . . . Kind of.

Wale   Good . . . Because I am quite taken by you, Ayamma.

He moves in even closer.

Ayamma (*shy*)   Is that from one of your films?

Wale   No. Just my own script.

Ayamma   Oh . . . Well . . . I do love your movies . . . Like I've told you, I can watch them over and over—

Wale   —And over and over again . . . I remember.

Ayamma   Oh.

Wale   I too, have something I have been wanting to do over . . . and over . . . and over again.

Ayamma   Oh . . . And what would that be?

Wale   This . . .

Wale *leans in and slowly traces several kisses behind* **Ayamma***'s ear and down her neck. It is smooth. It is sexy—just like* **Wale***.* **Ayamma** *becomes lost in the sensuality of it all. After a beat, the teapot begins to whistle, jolting* **Ayamma** *and* **Wale** *back into reality.*

Wale (*smiles*)   It appears the tea is ready.

Ayamma   Uh, yes.

Beat.

Dede (*O.S.*)   AYAMMA? WHY HAS IT GONE SILENT? WHAT IS GOING ON?

Ayamma *and* **Wale** *laugh again. She turns off the kettle and pours a cup for both herself and for* **Wale***.*

Ayamma   I hope you like ginger tea with extra honey. Gives it a very spicy and sweet taste.

Wale   Hmm. I'm more of a milk and sugar kind of guy. Nothing too fancy.

Ayamma   Just try it. You might like it.

She hands **Wale** *a cup.*

Wale   A toast—

Ayamma   —Ah! Please keep in mind your last toast did not work out very well.

Wale   No, this will be good: To the . . . No . . . To our future.

Ayamma   Cheers.

They clink cups, blow and then take a small sip.

Wale   Not bad. I could get used to this.

They continue to sip. Lights shift.

Scene Ten: Okafor Travel Agency

Dede *and* **Ayamma** *are at the office.* **Dede** *is doing her usual work: lounging around and watching TV and* **Ayamma** *is busying herself with sorting files. The* Adenikeh *theme song plays.*

Adenikeh (V.O./O.S) *(on television)*   I would like to thank my guests Gbenga Ezie and Fayola Ogunleye! Can't wait to see what you both have in store for us. And please tune in tomorrow for an all new episode of *Adenikeh*! Thank you for letting me bring love into your home! Take care, everyone!

Dede *lowers the television volume.*

Dede   Hmmm, Fayola . . . Well, she can star in as many movies as she wants, but she is not fooling anyone with that wig! And I know they say TV adds ten pounds, but clearly she's been enjoying her rice and stew too much. That's all I'm saying.

Ayamma   Dede, you don't have to say those things to make me feel better. I told you, I am over it. I am fine now.

Dede   Well, you better be fine. If I was dating Wale Owusu, I would be running all over Lagos banging a drum shouting it to anyone who will listen.

Ayamma   Well that is where you and I differ.

Dede   Listen, if you ask me—

Ayamma   —Which I am not—

Dede   —This is better than that stupid movie. You get the prize.
In real life.

Ayamma   He is not a prize, Dede.

Dede   He is to me . . .

Ayamma *shakes her head.*

Dede   God, what are his lips like, eh? And speak slowly. Slower
than you did the last time. I want to envision how they would feel
on mine.

Ayamma   You realize that it is very sick to lust after your sista's
man.

Dede   Ohhh! So he is your man now?

Ayamma   No, I did not say that. I am just saying that if MAYBE
something happens with us, you will have to back off.

Dede   You know I am just joking around.

Ayamma   It is bad enough I have to think about him and Fayola,
I do not want to have to worry about you the same.

Dede   Oh please. You have nothing to worry about with me. I can
barely look at him, much less talk to him. You have seen it.

Ayamma   I have.

Dede   And quit worrying about Fayola. I told you that I (*winks*)
took care of her.

Ayamma   Dede please.

Dede   Listen, I cannot speak for my powers. Perhaps they just
work in a different way. But when they hit, they hit like a lightning
bolt striking the sand. Sharp and fast! . . . I'm telling you.

Ayamma (*sucks teeth*)   Okay, Dede.

The phone rings. **Dede** *answers, much to* **Ayamma**'s *surprise.*

Dede   Oh, maybe it's Wale! (*On phone.*) Thank you for calling Okafor Travels. This is Dede, how may I help you? . . . Oh, this is who? . . . For true? . . . Okay, hold on one moment. (*To* **Ayamma**.) It's for you.

Ayamma   Who is it?

Dede   Gbenga Ezie.

Ayamma   What? Why would he be calling for me?

Dede   I don't know.

Ayamma   Well, I do not want to talk to him.

Dede   Ayamma, quit being so stubborn.

Ayamma   They are already a week into filming the movie. What does he have to say to me?

Dede   Obviously something if he's going to call you here at your workplace . . . Maybe a new movie? Take the call, Ayamma, ah!

Ayamma *rolls her eyes and relents.*

Dede (*under breath*)   So foolish, oh.

Ayamma (*attitude*)   Hello, this is Ayamma speaking . . . Yes, hello Mr. Ezie, how are you? . . . Mmm hmmm . . . Yes . . . (*Shocked.*) Excuse me? . . . Yes . . . Yes. I can do that . . . Okay. Thank you. Bye now.

Ayamma *hangs up the phone. She is still in shock.*

Pause.

Dede   Uh, hello?!

Pause.

Dede   Helllllllllllo? What? What did he say.

Ayamma   Fayola was in an accident.

Dede (*shocked*)   You say what?!

Ayamma   She's okay, she tripped on a pot hole and broke her leg.

Dede (*relieved*)   Oh . . . And?

Ayamma   And he can't have his leading lady hopping around on crutches . . . So he wanted to know if I was still free. He'd like me to take the part . . . I'm playing Comfort! Ahhh!

They both celebrate.

Dede   Ahhh! You see, and you were judging my skills. (*Gloating.*) Her legs, of course! They are her money maker . . . I'm so good, I don't even know what to do with myself. I mean, I hate that I have to be the one to tell you these things, but as your older sister by two years, it is clear that I am a fountain of wisdom and power. Now you see why I have to rest all the time at work, because my spirit is just exhausted. But what did I say? When it hits, it hits! . . . Well, at least this time.

Ayamma   THIS time.

Dede *and* **Ayamma**   Ahhhhh!

They celebrate again. Lights shift.

Scene Eleven: *Adenikeh* TV Studio

Lights fade and the theme to Adenikeh *fades out.*

Adenikeh   Welcome back. We are sitting here with acclaimed film director Gbenga Ezie, Nollywood darling Fayola Ogunleye and the gorgeous, Wale Owusu.

The audience claps and cheers as **Wale**, **Gbenga** *and* **Fayola** *smile and wave at the audience.*

Adenikeh   We're here talking about their latest film *The Comfort Zone* where, as I understand it, after the nationwide open call, where close to 5,000 girls from ALL over Africa auditioned for the role of Comfort, our next guest was the last to come in. Audience, please help me welcome Nigeria's bright new star—Ayamma Okafor.

Light claps from the audience as **Ayamma** *enters, waving excitedly.*

Ayamma   Thank you so much, Adenikeh. My sister and I never miss your show—you don't know.

Adenikeh   Oh, well . . . Thank you! So tell me, were you just a ball of nerves when you auditioned for the movie?

Ayamma   Yes! I was so nervous—I mean, this was the opportunity of a lifetime.

Gbenga   And she was incredible. I knew it before she even uttered a word.

Fayola   Yes, she made quite the entrance.

Wale   When you watch the film, you'll see—she's very . . . special.

Wale *winks at* **Ayamma***. She blushes.*

Ayamma   Thank you.

Adenikeh   Now, is it true that Gbenga plucked you from obscurity when you were working at some unknown, small, family business?

Ayamma   Yes, yes. That is why I really wanted to impress Mr. Ezie.

Adenikeh   Well, it appears you have impressed more than just him! Critics are calling your work (*reads her cue card*) "the kind of smashing film debut that actors dream about" . . . "You cannot take your eyes off of her." . . . "She is not a star, she is a galaxy!" . . . Wow! I mean, how do you feel hearing those compliments about your work?

Ayamma   Overwhelmed. I'm just glad that Mr. Ezie took a chance on me.

Gbenga   Hey, sometimes a chance is all you need.

Adenikeh   Now everyone is saying that this movie is going to change the face of Nigeria. What does that feel like for you all? A dream come true?

Fayola/Ayamma/Wale   Yes / Oh absolutely! / For sure.

Gbenga   And you know, that's the funny thing about dreams: sometimes they actually become a reality . . .

Fayola   And sometimes, they don't . . . But that's how it goes in Nollywood.

Adenikeh (*to camera/audience*)   Mmm. Wise words from a wise woman . . . And now, without further adieu, here is the exclusive trailer for the highly anticipated new movie *The Comfort Zone*.

A screen drops and we quickly fade into the trailer for The Comfort Zone.

Ext. Open Road—Nigeria—Day

We see two young children, a little boy and little girl, age ten, playing soccer in the road together.

Movie Trailer Voice (*West African accent*)   Comfort and James grew up in a world where nothing could keep them apart.

Cut to:

Ext. Secondary School House—Nigeria—Day

Teenage James and Comfort walking out from school together laughing holding hands.

Movie Trailer Voice   Through school, life and family, they always knew their love would see them through.

Cut to:

Int. Romantic Restaurant—Nigeria—Night

"James" and "Comfort" sit at a table eating stew and rice together. They drink wine and laugh (small beat). Then suddenly—

Wale (*as James*)   "Comfort, I have to tell you something."

Ayamma (*as Comfort*)   "Yes, James, anything."

Wale   "I have been accepted to an educational program in America. They only accept three people in the whole world and they have chosen me."

Ayamma   "Oh James, how long will you be gone?

Wale   "I am unsure. But just make me this one promise: that you will hold on to our love."

Ayamma   "I will do anything for you."

Cut to:

Ext. Street—America—Day

James is walking the streets holding an American flag and meets Rose (who is on crutches).

Movie Trailer Voice   But, in time, the reality of life sets in and unexpected things happen.

Fayola (*as Rose; bad country accent; on crutches*)   "Excuse me. Are you lost? Can I help you find your way?"

Wale (*as James*)   "I don't know, maybe."

Quick montage set to melodramatic African music:

Ext. Park—America—Day

James and Rose walking through the park in love.

Int. Comfort's House—Nigeria—Day

Comfort sitting in the window sill staring at a phone beside her willing it to ring.

Ext. Church Steps—America—Day

James and Rose kissing after their wedding.

Int. or Ext. Comfort's House—Nigeria—Day

Comfort sweeping her home in Nigeria, looking at a picture of her and James together: happier times.

Ext. Park—America—Day

James and Rose admiring their newborn baby while having a picnic in the park.

Int. Comfort's House—Nigeria—Day

Comfort receiving a letter in the mail that reads "return to sender."

Movie Trailer Voice   But what happens when you are reunited with your one true love:

Ext. Nigerian Marketplace—Nigeria—Day

James and Comfort bump into each other at the marketplace.

Wale (*as James*)   "I cannot believe this"

Ayamma   "James, is that really you?"

Movie Trailer Voice   But you have already married someone else?

James slips off his wedding band and puts it into his pocket.

Cut to:

Ext. Comfort's House

Comfort is sitting out front of her house, drinking, and fanning herself.

Fayola   "Excuse me, is this the residence of James Adegbola?"

Ayamma   "And who is asking for him?"

Fayola   "His wife. From America."

Dramatic music swells and the camera focuses on the stare down between Rose and Comfort.

Movie Trailer Voice   Find out what happens, when love is put the test. Will it land in hot water . . .

Jump cut to:

Rose (on crutches) crying.

Jump cut to:

James' confusion.

Jump cut to:

Comfort crying.

Jump cut to:

James embracing Rose.

Jump cut to:

then James embracing Comfort.

Cut to:

I/E. Nigeria

Rose, in her wedding dress, James and Comfort stare into the camera—brooding.

Movie Trailer Voice   Or will it stay in . . . THE COMFORT ZONE. On home video this year. This is a Nollywood Dreams Production.

The screen fades to black. End of play.

School Girls;
Or, The African Mean Girls Play

JC—thank you for fighting for me and this play. It worked.
Love you, girl.

Characters

Note: All characters are of West African descent and are to be played by African and/or Black actors. Thank you.

Paulina Sarpong *(pronounced Paul-lee-nah Saar-pong)—eighteen years old; most popular girl in school and knows it. She is beautiful, talented, vindictive yet somehow lovable.*

Ericka Boafo *(pronounced Bwah-foh)—eighteen years old; light/fair skin. Note: should be played by a fair-skinned biracial (Black and White) woman. She is a transfer student and is new to the school. She is enchanting, sweet, and elusive. Good singer.*

Ama *(pronounced Ahh-mah)—eighteen years old; the sensible, smart one of Paulina's pack who has the honor of being her best friend. Her loyalty to Paulina is starting to fray and she has to work up toward being the girl who is not afraid to say it like she means it.*

Nana *(pronounced Nah-nah)—sixteen years old; the quiet, simple, and sensitive one of Paulina's pack. She never means any harm and strives to do the right thing. She struggles with her love of food and snacks.*

Mercy—*sixteen years old; the witty sidekick to Gifty who will do and say anything to stay a member of Paulina's pack.*

Gifty—*sixteen years old; the "Frick" to Mercy's "Frack"; loves being part of Paulina's pack and will do anything to be considered cool.*

Headmistress Francis—*forties; the headmistress of Aburi Girls Boarding School; loves her students and will do whatever she can to both uplift and protect them.*

Eloise Amponsah *(pronounced Amm-pone-saah)—forties; Extremely poised and well-mannered former Miss Ghana 1976. She is now a recruiter for the Miss Ghana pageant. She speaks with a slightly affected British accent and prides herself on always being a lady.*

Setting and Time

Aburi (Ehh-bree) Girls Boarding School—located in the Aburi Mountains in central Ghana. The year is 1986.

Playwright's Note

In 2011, the Miss Ghana pageant officials, in an attempt to become the first West African country to have a viable and perhaps winning contestant in the Miss Universe pageant, named Yayra Erica Nego (an American-born and Minnesota-raised biracical woman) the winner of the Miss Ghana pageant. Officials claimed that her father was from the Volta region of Ghana (a region that is considered extremely obscure and rarely have people ever emigrated from there) but never confirmed his name or whereabouts before procuring her as a contestant for the Miss Ghana pageant. She beat out two of Ghana's most famous models at the time. Erica went on to the Miss Universe pageant that year where she did not place.

I thought that story was pretty damn interesting . . . So I wrote a play inspired by it.

Part One

*Breakfast at Aburi Girls School. The "crew": **Paulina**, **Ama**, **Nana**, **Mercy**, and **Gifty** sit at a lunch table. They are The Popular Crew and everyone knows it.*

Paulina   Seriously, Nana? After all I've said, you are still eating porridge?

Mercy   Yeah, is this your idea of a diet?

Nana   Well, it's a smaller portion.

Paulina   Are you determined to look like a cow?

All Girls (*except* **Nana**)   Ha! / A cow! / Farm animals!

The girls all giggle.

Paulina   Listen, Nana, I don't know how many times I have to say it:

*Snaps at **Mercy** to cue her.*

Mercy   "We have a reputation to maintain."

Gifty   "To stay fit."

Mercy   "Looking fine-fine."

Gifty   "All the time."

Paulina   Listen, I get it—you never got to eat what you wanted when you were younger—

Mercy   But you can't make up for lost time now.

Gifty   Yeah, the time is lost.

Paulina   So . . . do you want to be fat-fat? Or fit and popular?

Mercy *and* **Gifty**   Yeah, choose your choice.

Nana   Umm . . . popular.

Paulina   Good . . . Then let me help you make smarter choices. I need an apple anyway.

Mercy   Oh, we can get it for you, Paulina.

Paulina   No, no, it's fine. I'm trying to burn some more calories.

She leaves.

Mercy   Sorry, Nana.

Gifty   Yeah, sorry.

Mercy   We just don't want her coming after us.

Nana   No, I get it.

Ama   She has been acting so crazy lately.

Mercy   I know—this pageant! She's always judging everything.

Gifty (*imitating* **Paulina**)   "You like your hair like that?"

Mercy   "Those shoes are hideous."

Gifty   "You know, girls . . . Apples are a very good source of fiber!"

Mercy   Like we know what fiber is!

Nana   She's just looking out for us. Like she always has.

Ama   Looking out for us? Please!

Marcy *and* **Gifty**   Oooh, yeah.

Mercy   I still can't believe you were able to forgive her, Ama.

Gifty   Forgiveness.

Mercy   Had that got back to your father

Gifty   A pastor

Mercy   Who knows what would have happened.

Gifty   Crucifixion!

Ama   Can we not bring that up right now?

Mercy   Fine.   **Ama**   Sorry.

Gifty   She's just acting up because her and Kofi broke up again.

Nana   No, she told me they're back together now.

Ama   Whatever. I can't keep up anymore.

Mercy   Well, she promised me and Gifty dresses for the audition. So I won't ruffle too many feathers before then.

Gifty   Feathers.

Ama (*to* **Mercy/Gifty**)   But your father can afford to get you and Gifty any dress you want already.

Mercy   But you know he won't get us frivolous things!

Gifty   And to him, dresses from America? Frivolous!

Mercy   We know we won't be picked, but we can at least look good.

Ama   Whatever. Paulina only made us all sign up to audition because Headmistress said there needed to be at least five names on the list.

Nana   But we could have a chance.

Ama   Please, Nana, no one ever stands a chance when it comes to Paulina.

Paulina *re-enters.*

Paulina   And don't you forget it!

All Girls   Paulina! / Welcome back! / We missed you.

Paulina (*hands* **Nana** *an apple*)   Here you are, Nana.

Nana   Oh, thanks, Paulina.

Paulina   I got you the smallest one. I can't say it enough, ladies: regulation is your friend.

Ama   Totally.

Mercy   Our friend.

Gifty   Our best friend. Other than you of course, Paulina.

Paulina   Awww, you are so sweet, Gifty.

Gifty   Thank you, Paulina.

Paulina (*takes a bite of her apple*)   You know, girls, apples are a very good source of fiber. My American cousins told me there is a parable there that says: "An apple a week, keeps you from being sick."

Nana (*takes a bite*)   Yeah . . . They're really good.

Gifty (*to* **Nana**)   They keep you from being sick.

Paulina   Portion control, Nana . . .

Nana *stops eating and puts the apple down.*

Paulina (*moving on*)   Ugh. I'm so tired this morning. Can you see it under my eyes?

(*Pulls down her "eye bags."*) Tired, right?

Mercy/Gifty/Ama   What?! No! / Are you kidding?! / You? Never!

Paulina   Really? Well, I was up all night writing a letter to my Kofi.

The girls all swoon.

Mercy   Oh, how is he? Is his training going well? I'm glad you're back together.

Gifty   Don't you miss him?

Paulina   Of course I miss him. But if I'm going to be married

Mercy/Gifty/Ama   Oooh/ Awww / Eh-eh, married where?

Paulina   Well, eventually be married to a potential football player, then I have to get used to us being away from each other.

Mercy   But he's planning to come to the big dance, yes?

Paulina   Of course! He can't wait. I am really looking forward to you all meeting him.

Ama   Oh, so he is definitely going to come this time? He's missed the last two.

Paulina   Because he was busy—like I said.

Ama   Right.

Mercy   And what about you, Ama? Is your Osei going to come?

Ama (*blushing*)   Yes, he is.

The girls all giggle (except **Paulina***).*

Mercy   I'm telling you, Ama, Osei is so fine.

Gifty   So fine!

Mercy   That skin, that smile, that body?!

Gifty   Perfect.

Mercy   You are a lucky one, eh.

Ama   Thanks, girls.

Paulina   Yes, well let's just hope he keeps his eyes fixed on you this time.

Ama   Pardon?

Paulina   Oh, I didn't want to make a big deal about it, but he was practically all over me at the last dance.

Ama   I didn't see any of that.

Paulina   Well, you wouldn't. He must be one of those slick ones—a womanizer.

Gifty (*confused about what to say*)   . . . Yeah . . . A womanizer . . .

Mercy (*let's change the subject*)   So, Paulina. Have you decided what you are going to wear for the Miss Ghana audition?

Gifty   Are you making a dress for yourself again? Your designs are so gorgeous.

Mercy   Or are you wearing something your cousins in America gave you? I can't believe how many options they sent.

Ama   Yeah, it was a lot.

Paulina   I know. Well, you know my Auntie Salo works at that high-class restaurant I was telling you about.

Mercy   Ah yes, White Castle.

Gifty   A castle with food.

Paulina   And she is always shopping for me at all the trendy American boutiques.

Primark. Wal-Mart. The list goes on. But since this is such a big moment in my life, she sent me an outfit purchased at the most famous retail place in all of New York City.

Mercy (*amazed*)   Where?   **Gifty**   Where is that?

Paulina   Chinatown!

Mercy/Nana/Gifty   Wow / Oh my goodness / There is a China in New York?!

Paulina   That's right, ladies. I will be wearing my very own Calvin Klean dress to the dance.

Mercy   Oh my goodness!

Gifty   I don't even know who that is!

Nana   I am so jealous of your life, Paulina.

Paulina   I know. I'm so blessed.

Ama   Yeah, you really are.

Paulina   Oh, Ama, don't worry. I know you can't afford to get a nice dress for yourself, so I'll let you wear one of my options. I'm sure one of them will fit you.

Ama   Uh, thanks, Paulina, but I think I'll be okay.

Paulina   Are you sure? I mean, you're my best friend and I really need you to look good, Ama.

An awkward beat.

Mercy (*trying to cool things down again*)   You are so thoughtful, Paulina! Giving us *all* dresses.

Gifty   What are we going to do without you when you and Ama graduate?

Paulina   I don't know. So take this last year to soak up my wisdom.

Ama   Or maybe you girls will be just fine on your own? Thinking for yourselves is not hard you know?

Mercy   Eh-eh. Think for myself?

Gifty   Why would I do that?

Paulina   And what is that supposed to mean, Ama?

Ama   I'm just saying that they are smart girls and they don't need to follow anyone—

Paulina   —I just think they appreciate that I protect them! Like how people make fun of Mercy because her rich daddy won't buy her new shoes.

Mercy   He's very . . . frugal.

Paulina   Or the way people talk about Gifty now that she's had to repeat her first year.

Gifty   Not cool.

Paulina   And Nana here: who ate lunch everyday by herself until I brought her into the group. Finally giving her some friends. Isn't that right, Nana?

Nana   Yes.

Ama   Look, Paulina, I'm not trying to start anything, okay?

Paulina   Are you sure? Look, you're not still mad about that thing are you? I thought we were over it.

Ama   I am . . . We are.

Paulina   Good.

Headmistress Francis *walks into the cafeteria.* **Paulina** *turns on her "public face" charm.*

Headmistress Francis   Oh, good morning, girls.

All Girls   Good morning, Headmistress.

Paulina   How are you this morning, Headmistress?

Headmistress Francis   I'm well, thank you. A bit busy this morning. We have a new student coming in today.

That's a surprise to everyone.

Ama   Really? We're already in our second week of school.

Headmistress Francis   I know. So I trust you all will help in getting her settled quickly, yes?

All Girls   Yes / Of course, Headmistress. / For sure.

Paulina   What a week we're having! We were just talking about how excited we all are about the Miss Ghana recruiter coming tomorrow. Isn't that right, ladies?

All Girls   Yes! / We can't wait! / I'm so nervous.

Mercy   How many girls will they be selecting?

Gifty   Is it true that it's only one?

Headmistress Francis   Yes, only one.

Gifty (*to* **Mercy**)   I told you!

Paulina   And if she wins that, then she'll go on to the Miss Global Universe pageant with girls from all over the world!

All Girls   Ahhh! / That is so amazing! / All over the world?! / Wow!

Headmistress Francis   Now, I am not a big fan of competitions myself, you know what I always say:

All Girls "Education is the only gift that no one can take away."

Headmistress Francis That's right. And I want you all to remember, that even if you are not selected, it is not the end of the world. God still loves you! Amen?

All Girls Amen.

Headmistress Francis Good.

Mercy But Paulina, you *are* going to be Miss Ghana 1986!

Nana Yes, of course! We all know that you are the most beautiful girl here at Aburi.

Ama Yeah . . .

Paulina (*coy*) Well . . .

Headmistress Francis Okay . . . now girls—

Mercy —And no one from West Africa has ever made it to the top of the Miss Global Universe pageant.

Headmistress Francis Is that so?

Gifty Yes! It is always some girl from South Africa or Ethiopia.

Nana Eh-eh! You remember when the winner from Namibia was a white?!

Headmistress Francis A white?

Ama Well, they said that she was born and raised there, so technically she is African.

Mercy Oh, so then it would be no problem if the winner of Miss Italy had black skin?

Gifty Oh please! You know there would be many problems with that—

Nana —She probably wouldn't even make it to the stage—

Mercy —That is what I am saying—

Ama —I'm just letting you know how they got around the rules!

Headmistress Francis —Okay, calm down, girls—

Nana —But you know what else I heard?!

All Girls What?!

Nana That this year's winner will accompany Bobby Brown to an American awards show!

Mercy/Gifty/Ama/Nana BOBBY BROWN! /Ahhh! / I would die!

Headmistress Francis Eh, girls! Inside voices please!

Mercy Oh my God, if I could listen to "Mr. Telephone Man" a million times a day, I would!

Gifty Me too!

Headmistress Francis Me three! That song is my JAM!

All Girls (*excitement that she knows the song*) AYYYYE! / HEADMISTRESS! / LOOK AT YOU, OH!

Headmistress *exits. The girls settle down.*

Nana Wow, Paulina. You will be in all the American magazines! Eating at fancy restaurants.

Mercy Rubbing elbows with famous people.

Gifty Elbows!

Paulina I know.

Ama Don't you think Kofi would mind?

Paulina Of course not. He would not want to interfere with my modeling career.

Ama You say what?

Paulina Modeling. That's the plan after I graduate you know. Become the next Iman. College is cute, but I'm thinking about my future realistically.

Mercy   Listen, I'm sure that Kofi is going to be very excited to tell everyone that he is with the most beautiful woman in Ghana . . .

Gifty   Ghana!

Mercy   Or in the whole world.

Gifty   Universe!

Paulina (*feigned humility*)   Ladies. Please.

Gifty   It is true! Who else could beat you?

Headmistress *re-enters the cafeteria with a new girl,* **Ericka.** *Everyone stares in shock.*

Headmistress Francis   Girls, I would like you all to meet Ericka Boafo. She has just transferred into Aburi.

Ericka   Hello, everyone.

All Girls   Hi.

Headmistress Francis   Ericka, this is Gifty, Paulina, Mercy, Ama, and Nana. Paulina and Ama here are in their last year as well.

Paulina   Welcome to Aburi, Ericka.

Ericka   Thank you.

Headmistress Francis   Ericka is joining us all the way from the States!

Mercy   The United States of America?

Gifty   So are you a white?

Headmistress Francis   Gifty!

Ericka   No, it's fine, Headmistress. I am a little pale. Clearly, I have been missing some of that good African sun.

All the girls, except **Paulina***, laugh. They like her already.*

Headmistress Francis   I'm sorry for the quick tour. I need to go and set up some classrooms—we're a bit short staffed today. But if you need anything, Ericka, please don't hesitate to ask.

Ericka   Thank you, Headmistress, but I'm sure I'll be fine.

Paulina   Yes, we'll take good care of her.

Headmistress Francis   Lovely. See you all soon.

She exits.

Paulina   Please, Ericka. Have a seat.

Ericka   Thank you.

The girls all move down to make room for **Ericka**. *A small beat of awkward silence as they all stare at her.*

Paulina   So . . . You're from America?

Ericka   Yes. Well, no. I mean . . . I'm Ghanaian.

I've just been living in the States for a while.

Paulina   Oh, well, that's exciting. I have some cousins who live there as well.

Ericka   Really? Where?

Paulina (*she doesn't know where*)   Like . . . all over.

Ama   Where did you live?

Ericka   I went to school in the Midwest area. Ohio.

Mercy   Ohio.

Gifty   I've never even heard of that one before.

Ericka   It's nothing special.

Nana   Aren't your cousins from New York, Paulina?

Gifty   Is that near Ohio?

Paulina   Yeah. They're in New York. And all over America. Like I said.

Ama And you're in your last year as well?

Ericka I am. I hope I haven't missed too much. I know you all started classes a week ago.

Ama I'm sure you'll catch up.

Ericka I appreciate Headmistress making an exception for me.

Paulina A special exception it seems. What do your parents do?

Ericka Oh, my dad has a company . . . A cocoa factory actually.

Ama Boafo? As in Boafo Cocoa Farms?

Ericka Yes, you know it?

The girls all know that company. They are impressed.

Mercy (*sotto voce*)   Oh, they make some *good* cocoa!

Gifty (*sotto voce*)   Chocolate.

Ama Yes, of course. My boyfriend works at that dairy farm.

Ericka He does? Oh you must be talking about, ummm . . .

Ama Osei (*Ohh-say*).

Ericka Right.

Ama You know him?

Ericka Not really, but I think I've seen him around.

Ama Osei says that your parents travel a lot—he rarely even sees them.

Ericka Yeah, he's right—they are always busy traveling. The schedule was becoming too much. Transferring schools all the time. So we decided that I should finish my schooling here in his hometown.

Paulina So when was the last time you were here?

Ericka I can't even tell you. So, forgive me. It's going to take me a while to get my accent and get used to the heat.

The girls all laugh. Except **Paulina**.

Mercy   I'm sorry, Ericka, but I have to ask: what did you use to get your hair that long?

Ericka   Oh, this is just natural.

Gifty   Wow. You are so lucky.

Ericka   Thanks but Headmistress scheduled my haircut for next week.

Paulina   I mean, mine is that long too. When I straighten it, you can see—

Nana   —I wish my hair was easier to manage.

Ericka   Well, I have tons of products you could try—a bunch of things that I got in America.

Nana   Ooh, like what? Hair grease?

Mercy   Oil?

Ama   Lotion?

Ericka   All of that. You girls should come to my dormitory and try them out. We can have a little makeover party or something.

Mercy   Oooh, a makeover party.

Gifty   A party to get made over!

Nana   Count me in!

Ama   Yeah, I want to try everything.

Gifty   Cause your stuff must be top quality!

Mercy   Clearly! Even the Caro Light they have in the States must be top shelf. You don't even have any blemishes!

Ericka   The what?

Mercy   You know? The cream.

Gifty   Bleaching cream.

Mercy   The ones they sell here will just burn your skin off.

Gifty   Fire.

Mercy   And they give really bad blisters.

Gifty   Nasty.

Ericka   Oh, well—

Mercy   —But I would love to try yours! It seems like it works really good.

Gifty   Quality.

Ericka   Oh, no. I don't use . . . I mean, this is just my natural tone.

Gifty   Wow. You really are blessed.

Mercy   Our other cousin has lighter skin too.

Gifty   She's albino!

Mercy   It's still light!

Gifty   Anyway, I can't wait for this party! Are you free after class today? Oooh! Do you have a boombox? The one I had broke down.

Ama   That thing never worked, Gifty.

Gifty   It did!

(*Under breath.*) You just had to hold the plug in place and it was fine . . .

Mercy (*under breath*)   Let it go, Gifty.

Ericka   I do have one actually! And I brought some new music with me too.

Mercy   Do you know of Bobby Brown?

Ericka   Are you kidding? I love him! I went to a New Edition concert last year.

All Girls   YOU DID?!

Ericka   Yeah, I even have a poster that he signed.

Mercy   Oh my goodness!

Gifty   He signed a poster!

Nana   And she has it!

All Girls   AHHH!

Paulina   You have to forgive them, Ericka. We don't always get such fancy new students like you in our school—with your music and lotions and makeup.

Mercy   All the things we need to look good for the recruiter!

Ericka   Recruiter?

Gifty   For the Miss Ghana pageant!

Ericka   Oh yeah! I saw that list in the front office. I signed up for it. Looks like fun!

Small beat. Uh oh.

Mercy (*trying to cut through the tension*)   It is going to be fun!

Nana (*without even thinking*)   And you can definitely be the next Miss Ghana.

Paulina (*to* **Nana**)   Oh really?

Nana   I mean—

Ericka   Yeah, I thought it might be a fun way to make some friends.

Paulina   Oh, so you are not really that interested?

Ericka   Well, I've never thought about beauty pageants before.

Ama   Surely someone has told you that you are perfect for modeling or something?

Ericka   I mean maybe once or twice.

Paulina   But now you are seriously thinking about it?

Ericka   I guess so.

Ama   It's just a pageant. What do you have to lose?

Paulina (*laughs*)   Well, other than to me. Obviously.

Ericka   Right . . .

Beat. Something's going on here.

Paulina   So do you have a boyfriend, Ericka?

Ericka   Not anymore—

Paulina   —Cause I do! Kofi. He's in Kumasi training with the Ghana Black Stars. He's a football player. He's even been to the World Cup.

Ericka   That's nice.

Mercy *and* **Gifty** (*sotto voce*)   World Cup?

Paulina   But you don't have a boyfriend, huh?

Ericka   I've just been focused on my studies and my extracurriculars.

Ama   Well, you should join the show choir. We're all in it. Well, it's just us. But it's really fun.

Ericka   Oh yeah?

Mercy   And sometimes Headmistress lets us pick our songs.

Gifty   Like the one we're working on now.

Mercy   We've been rehearsing all week!

Gifty   And she is letting us perform it for the recruiter as part of the auditions.

Mercy   Since we all have solos!

Gifty   Which is special—since Paulina usually gets those.

Paulina   Actually, I'm the *lead* soloist. For the past two years.

Ericka   Oh that's nice. You must be really good.

Paulina   I am. Headmistress likes to make everyone feel like they have a fair chance, but we all know I'm the best. These girls sing like hyenas.

She laughs. No one joins her—or if they do, it's half-hearted. The school bell chimes.

Ericka   I should probably get to class. I just wish I knew where I was going though.

Mercy   Oh, what room are you looking for?

Ericka   138—Advanced Algebra?

Ama   Oh, I have that class too. I'll show you the way.

Ericka   Oh great, thanks. If nothing else, I'm glad I know how to get to the most important place on campus.

Nana   Where is that?

Ericka   The cafeteria! I'm so greedy. I already can't wait for lunch.

The girls laugh. **Ericka**, **Mercy**, **Gifty**, *and* **Ama** *all walk off to class.* **Paulina** *pulls* **Nana** *to the side before she can follow after them.*

Paulina   So, Nana, have you forgotten where your loyalty lies?

Nana   What? You know I am always nice with everyone.

Paulina   I don't give a shit about nice! There's no room for that in this group, you hear me?

Nana *is silent.*

(*Snaps fingers.*) Hello? Do you hear me? Or do you have food stuffed in your ears too, you fucking cow!

Nana   Yes, I hear you.

Paulina   Now, since you keep getting caught with snacks in class, you have another detention after school today, yes?

Nana   Yes.

Paulina   Good. Because I need you to sneak into Headmistress's files and pull Ericka's out for me.

Nana   What?!

Paulina   You heard me.

Nana   Paulina, I can't do that. Do you know how much trouble I could get in if Headmistress found out?

Paulina   Do I look like I care?

Nana   What do you even need with her files anyway?

Paulina   That's none of your business.

Nana   Well, you're going to have to ask someone else because I can't do that, Paulina. Headmistress has already warned me that if I get any more detentions, it is going to affect me getting into college. And you know how much that means to me. I would be the first in my family.

Paulina   Well, it obviously doesn't mean enough.

She reaches into **Nana**'s *top and pulls out a small bread roll.*

Nana   Paulina, no. Please. Give it back!

Paulina (*mocking*)   "Oh, Paulina, please, just let me eat. I just want to go to college!" Give me a fucking break, okay?!

She throws the bread on the floor.

Nana (*looks down in shame*)   I'm just hungry.

Paulina   Then eat . . . I'll just tell Headmistress about all the places you're stashing food. Then you'll get more detentions. And maybe expelled. And I know you don't want to be sent back to your mother with the way she likes to starve you. I mean, I can't blame her. I'd be ashamed if I had a fat ass daughter too.

Nana   Paulina, please. I can't do that—

Paulina   But you can avoid all of that strife, if you just get me Ericka's files. Like I told you to do the first damn time. Do we have an understanding now?

Nana (*eventually*)   Yes.

Paulina   Good. Oh, and don't get caught!

She walks off. After a moment, **Nana** *picks up the bread and stuffs it back in her shirt.*

Part Two

Headmistress Francis *sits at a lunch table in the cafeteria. She is going over some papers.* **Eloise**, *elegantly dressed, enters.*

Eloise (*slightly affected British accent*)   Francis Adwoa (Ah-joo-ah) Frimpong! Look at you!

Headmistress Francis   Eloise?

Eloise   I asked some students where I could find you and they said the cafeteria—

Headmistress Francis   —Yes, I'm just doing a bit of food inventory—

Eloise   —Of course you are. Oh, Franny. Come here! It's so good to see you!

An awkward hug.

Headmistress Francis   Yes. Quite the surprise.

Eloise   Whew, let me just catch my breath for second. I can't tell you the last time I have been up here in the Aburi mountains.

Headmistress Francis   Ah yes, it is definitely a workout.

Eloise   I can't believe we used to race up these hills every day! Feels like a hundred years ago, right?

Headmistress Francis   Sometimes . . .

Eloise   . . . Right.

Headmistress Francis   Pardon me, Eloise . . . but what are you doing here?

Eloise   Darling, I'm one of the recruiters for the Miss Ghana pageant.

Headmistress Francis   Oh, well isn't that a coincidence? We weren't expecting you until tomorrow.

Eloise   Yes, I know. But Aburi was the last school on my list, so I decided to come up earlier, go see my mum and some family—make a trip of it, you know? I haven't been back home in over ten years. Can you believe that?

Headmistress Francis   Yes I can.

Eloise   Anyway, I am so excited to be a recruiter this year. I feel very committed to finding a winning girl. You know—and I don't mean to brag—

Headmistress Francis   You? Of course not—

Eloise   —But if one of my recruits becomes Miss Ghana 1986, I will get a big promotion!

Headmistress Francis   Really?

Eloise   And you know what that means?

Headmistress Francis   Uhh, a bigger crown?

Eloise   No, it means big, big, big money! For both myself, the winner *and* a generous donation to the school—in this case, Aburi.

Headmistress Francis   Oh, I was not aware of that.

Eloise   I know that love. It's my job to tell you.

Headmistress Francis   That would be wonderful. Things have become a bit tight around here. I am managing but, you know, we could always use some help.

Eloise   Yes, I heard about girls testing pretty low in recent years, budget cuts, missionaries pulling their funding.

Headmistress Francis   We're managing. Trust me.

Eloise   Of course you are. Getting a few girls to work off their detentions with manual labor, eh? Headmistress Mary used to pull those same stunts when we were students here.

Headmistress Francis   Oh no, I'm just trying to teach the girls responsibility and—

Eloise   Oh, don't take offense, Franny! It was a joke. But seriously, if we find the right girl here: She wins. I win. And Aburi Girls School gets a big old paycheck.

Doesn't that sound great?

Headmistress Francis   It does.

Eloise   God only knows how much of your own personal money you have poured into this place.

Headmistress Francis   I love this school, Eloise. I don't mind the sacrifice.

Eloise   Awww . . .

(*Moving on.*) But, let's get to the matter at hand, eh? The girls.

Headmistress Francis   Well, they are all very excited.

Eloise   I remember when I was first discovered. Selling mangos at my mother's fruit stand when a recruiter just spotted me. It was a wondrous time in my life. That is, until the day I was crowned Miss Ghana of course.

Headmistress Francis   And you represented our country with much pride.

Eloise   And I hope to give some lucky young lady here the same chance . . . You know, it's funny because, as I was passing through, I happened to notice a lovely young lady.

Headmistress Francis   Oh?

Eloise   She is absolutely gorgeous. Ye', tall, brownish hair, lovely shape . . .

(*Eventually.*) Fair skinned.

Headmistress Francis   Ah, you must be talking about Ericka. She has just transferred into the school.

Eloise   Well, she is absolutely perfect for the pageant. As I said, I have turned over every rock and shook down every bush in Ghana it seems—honestly, I was getting desperate. But alas, God provides!

Headmistress Francis   All the time.

Eloise   Now she's a girl who can actually stand a chance against the likes of beauty queens from Spain, Brazil, France or Colombia.

Headmistress Francis   Well, yes, she's lovely, but I think many of my girls would.

Eloise   You know . . . It has become clear that MGU judges are fond of girls who have a more universal and commercial look.

Headmistress Francis   So . . . You are saying what exactly?

Eloise   That . . . we are just looking for girls that fall on the other end of the African skin spectrum.

Headmistress Francis   Okay, wait a minute. Eloise . . . How can you—of all people—co-sign with that?!

Eloise   Ummm . . . Big money! Big promotion! One step closer to owning the Miss Ghana pageant. Something a woman has never done!

Headmistress Francis   Oh please, this isn't about women's equality, this is about you! And I'm not going to have my girls used as pawns for your nonsense.

Eloise (*a bit more tart*)   Hey, hey! This pageant is not nonsense. It is an amazing opportunity for a girl from our country to travel the world and represent Ghana. I feel insulted that you would doubt my efforts. The MGU platform is a highly respected one.

Headmistress Francis   Platform?! Please!

Eloise   Listen, Francis—

Headmistress Francis   —You haven't changed one bit since secondary school. If it doesn't benefit you, who cares!

Eloise   That's right! And look at what that attitude has afforded me, darling! I'm Miss Ghana 1966. And here you are, still trying to keep up with the popular girls.

Headmistress Francis   And here you are, still trying to be one.

Paulina *walks into the cafeteria.*

Paulina   Oh, uh, good afternoon, Headmistress.

Headmistress Francis   Paulina, what are you doing out of class?

Paulina   Sister Donkor was not feeling well, so she dismissed us a few minutes early . . . Hello!

Eloise (*curt*)   Hello.

Headmistress Francis   Ah yes, Paulina. This is Eloise Amponsah: Miss Ghana 1966. She's this year's recruiter for the Miss Ghana pageant.

Paulina   Wow! Miss Ghana 1966! In the flesh! I can't believe it.

Eloise   Oh thank you, dear. Paulina, you said?

Paulina   Yes. Paulina Sarpong. I am in my last year here at Aburi.

Eloise   How lovely.

Paulina   We were not expecting you until tomorrow.

Eloise   Oh, well, I was just so anxious to see what Aburi had to offer, I couldn't wait.

Paulina (*here's her chance—very rehearsed and polished*)   I see. Well, I believe that it has always been my calling to do something influential. If I was chosen to be Miss Ghana, God will use me as a vessel to show the world how beautiful our country is and change the stereotypes of how Africans are perceived.

Eloise   Thank you . . . for that.

Paulina   You're welcome.

Headmistress Francis   Eh, Paulina, please tell Miss Amponsah more about your achievements here at school.

Paulina   Ah yes, well, I am very involved: I'm on the debate team, the table-tennis club and I am the lead soloist in the show choir. I'm also in a long-term relationship with a Ghana Black Star football player.

Eloise   Ooh, an athlete. Hold on to that one.

Paulina   Oh, I plan to. I know Kofi is my true love.

Headmistress Francis   Personally, I think Paulina would make for a great contestant in the pageant.

Eloise   Sure.

(*To* **Paulina**.) How tall are you, love?

Paulina   Oh, I can be any height you need me to be with the right pair of high-heeled shoes.

Eloise (*small dismissive laugh*)   And I can see you don't have a problem with your weight—

Headmistress Francis   Miss Amponsah—

Eloise   —These things are important to note, Headmistress.

Paulina   Well, I work out nearly every day and always try to eat appropriately.

Eloise   Oh, you are ahead of the game because, trust me, it doesn't get any easier when you are my age.

Paulina   Which cannot be a day over twenty-five. Surely you were too young to compete the first time around.

Eloise (*slightly flattered*)   Awww . . . How cute.

Headmistress Francis   I have to say, Miss Amponsah, I think you might be looking at your next Miss Ghana right here. See how she knows all the right things to say.

A school bell chimes.

Eloise   Ah . . . saved by the bell. Hmm . . . Anyway, I look forward to seeing what you and the rest of the girls have to offer when I'm back tomorrow.

Paulina   Me too. And again, it really was such an honor meeting you.

Eloise   Thank you, love. Well, let me get going now.

Headmistress Francis   Here, let me show you out, Miss Amponsah.

She and **Eloise** *exit as* **Nana** *enters the cafeteria.*

Nana   Good afternoon, Headmistress.

Headmistress Francis   Hello, Nana.

Nana   I was just about to head to the front office. You still need me to sort all of those records by the end of the day, yes?

Headmistress Francis   Uh . . . yes. But let me just see this guest out.

Nana   Yes, Headmistress.

Headmistress *and* **Eloise** *exit.* **Nana** *and* **Paulina** *are by themselves.*

Paulina (*awkward beat*)   So . . . were you able to—

Nana (*reaches into her book sack and pulls out a folder*)   Here.

Paulina   Great.

Nana *stares at* **Paulina** *as she starts to look through the files.*

Paulina (*noticing* **Nana**)   You can go now.

Nana *begins to leave.*

Paulina   Oh and Nana?

Nana   Yes?

Paulina   I've decided . . . you can't be a part of the group anymore. You're not really mixing with our . . . aesthetic. Come check in with me when you've dropped about fifteen to twenty pounds, okay? . . . Good luck.

Nana *is about to leave again, but stops herself.*

Nana   You know what, Paulina . . .

Paulina (*sighs—can't be bothered*)   What?

Nana   You're not as special as you think you are!

Paulina   I'm not?

Nana   No! You're not. And I can't believe that I used to feel lucky that I was your friend!

Small beat.

That I was actually proud that you claimed me. But you know what? I am lucky. Because I will never, ever be you!

Paulina (*dismissive*)   Nana . . . Of course you won't.

Nana *runs off as* **Ericka** *enters the cafeteria.* **Paulina** *is busy reading the file and doesn't immediately notice* **Ericka** *walk in.*

Ericka   Hey, Paulina.

Paulina (*stuffs the folder in her bag*)   Hi . . . What are you doing here?

Ericka   Just waiting for the girls. They told me to meet them here so we could walk over to the dorm together.

Paulina   Oh, that's right. Your little "makeover party."

Ericka   . . . Yeah . . . You can come too you know? Open invitation.

Paulina   No, I'm okay. I have more important things to do.

Ericka   Well, if you change your mind, you can always—

Paulina   I won't.

Ericka   . . . Okay.

Silence. Beat. Neither of them knows what to do. **Ericka** *takes a bar of chocolate out of her bag.*

Want some chocolate?

Paulina   No . . . Calories.

Ericka   Right.

Paulina Also, you should know that any sort of sweet is not allowed on campus or in the dormitories. It's considered contraband.

Ericka Oh . . . I thought we all just knew to keep it a secret.

Paulina Secrets, eh? Is that your thing?

Ericka No . . . But it's just chocolate.

Paulina Right. Your daddy's cocoa. Do you have an endless supply?

Ericka Not really.

Paulina I've driven past that property. Nice mansion.

Ericka Didn't spend much time there.

Paulina Ah, yes. America. Ohio. Don't you think your friends miss you?

Ericka I don't know. I had a pretty small circle.

Paulina I know the feeling . . . It's not like we just let anyone into our group.

Ericka *shifts.*

Ericka Oh . . . Is there a test you need to pass or something?

Paulina (*amused*) Listen . . . Ericka. You're new here, so let me help you understand some things: I have been running this school for a long time. Nothing and no one crosses me.

Ericka Okay.

Paulina And no one cares about your makeup, or music and fancy American things.

Ericka Clearly you do.

Paulina Excuse me?

Ericka You're the one who keeps bringing it up. Why do you care so much?

Paulina   I don't.

Ericka   You sure about that?

Paulina   Very.

Ericka   Listen, Paulina—I don't know what your problem is, but I'm not afraid of you, okay? It's going to take a lot more than some empty threats to shake me.

Paulina   No threats here. Just a warning.

Ericka   Sure.

Ama, **Mercy**, *and* **Gifty** *enter the cafeteria.*

Mercy *and* **Gifty**   Hi / Hey, Paulina.

Ama   Ericka! You ready to head over to the dorm?

Mercy *and* **Gifty**   Makeover party!

Paulina *sucks teeth loudly.*

She pushes past **Ama**, **Mercy**, *and* **Gifty** *to exit.*

Ama   What's her problem now?

Ericka   Not sure.

Mercy   Probably another one of her mood swings.

Ama (*rolls eyes*)   Always something with her.

Gifty   Well, let's go! I'm ready for this makeover party!

Mercy   Can't wait to see your dress options, Ericka!

Gifty   Honestly, we never really liked the ones that Paulina's aunt sent anyway.

Ericka   Is that the one who works at White Castle?

Ama *and* **Ericka** *laugh.* **Mercy** *and* **Gifty** *are confused.*

Mercy *and* **Gifty**   What?

Ama   Ericka told me about that place and, you guys, it is *far* from being a castle.

Mercy   Whaaaaat?

Gifty   No?! For true?!

Ama   They sell fast food there.

Ericka   Burgers and fries.

Mercy *and* **Gifty**   Like McDonald's?

Ericka   But not . . .

Ama   Oh . . . And Chinatown . . .

Ericka   All they sell there are knockoffs.

Mercy *and* **Gifty**   Knockoffs?

Ama   It's all fake! But Ericka has the real stuff.

Ericka   Calvin Klein. From Macy's department store.

Mercy   Woooooow.   **Gifty**   A store with departments.

Ericka   That's right. And you girls are going to look amazing!

Mercy   Wow. Ericka, it's like you were sent from heaven.

Gifty   A dress angel.

Ericka   Oh, come on.

Gifty   It's true. We are going to kill this audition.

Mercy   Yeah. And we have the list of sample questions that the recruiter might ask. I'm feeling very nervous about that section.

Ericka   Oh, come on, Mercy. It can't be that bad? Let's just practice one, yeah?

Gifty   Yesss! Rehearsal! This is great. (*To* **Ericka**.) Okay, so you be the host and we'll be the audience. Here, sit, Ama.

Ericka   Okay . . . You ready?

Mercy   No . . .

Gifty   You got this, cousin!

Ericka (*reads card*)   "So, if you could be either fire or water, what would you be and why?"

Mercy   Well . . . I am a human being and I do not know how it is to be fire or water. And for that reason, I really do not have an answer to this because, as you see, I am a human being.

I am a girl who has emotions and fire and water do not. So . . .

All the girls laugh.

Ericka   So . . . we'll practice a bunch of times tonight.

Mercy   Good. I'm going to need it.

Ama   And those questions are silly anyway, Mercy.

Gifty   *And* it doesn't matter how we answer the questions, because the recruiter will be too focused on our amazing dresses!

Ericka   That's right. So let's head over to my dorm and pick some looks!

All Girls   Yes! Makeover party!

Ericka   You girls want some chocolate?

All Girls   Oooh! Yeah!

They all laugh and head out excitedly.

Part Three

Paulina *enters the cafeteria to her own fanfare. She's dressed in a lovely dress, pageant ready.*

Paulina "And now, please welcome, Miss Ghana 1986 contestant, Paulina Sarpong"

(To herself.) And applause, applause, applause. Okay, then remember to stand straight, smile and look like you're having an amazing time.

(Plastic smile as she reads the card.) What would you do to change the image of Ghana if you were selected to be in the Miss Global Universe pageant?

(To herself.) "Should I be crowned, it will be" . . . no, "I will make it my mission to become influential in our political government" . . . no, "our political community to make Ghana stand out as an African nation that has thrived since our freedom" . . . "Our independence" . . . Yeah, that's good. Look confident. Be confident. You got this, Paulina. This is yours. This. Is. Yours.

She looks around, pulls out a small container of lotion and rubs it on her face; it stings, but she continues to rub it in anyway.

Nana *sees* **Paulina** *putting on the cream, but makes sure she's out of* **Paulina***'s sight. After a moment,* **Nana** *enters. She is dressed in her Sunday best as well. She looks at* **Paulina** *and then moves to sit at a table away from her.*

Paulina   Nana.

Nana   Paulina.

Silence.

Ready for the pageant?

Paulina   I've been ready.

Nana   Sure.

Silence.

Paulina   Look at you . . . Your dress is actually . . . pretty nice.

Nana   I know.

Silence.

. . . You know . . . My hands are a little dry. Do you have any cream?

Paulina   No.

Nana   You sure?

Ericka, **Ama**, **Mercy**, *and* **Gifty** *enter the cafeteria laughing and carrying on. They are all dressed in their Sunday best as well.* **Ericka** *and* **Paulina** *look the best by far.*

Ericka   Don't worry, Mercy. Your hair looks great!

Mercy   Oh God, I'm so nervous.

Gifty (*spotting* **Nana**)   Hey, Nana!

Ama   You look so pretty!

All Girls   Yes! / Hey, Nana! / Look at you! / Eh heh!

Nana   Thanks, girls.

Paulina (*sarcasm*)   Heh . . . Pretty.

Mercy *and* **Gifty**   This girl! / Heh—this one here.

Ama   Paulina.

Paulina   Awww . . . Look at you girls.

(*Amused.*) I'm sure you'll get points for effort.

Ama   And look at you, Paulina?! That knockoff Calvin Klean looks great.

The girls snicker.

Paulina   Actually, this is a new designer. I like to keep up with the hottest fashions.

Ama   Oh really?

Paulina   Yeah, you know I'm a trendsetter.

Mercy   Here she goes. Still telling lies!

Gifty   Running her mouth again!

Ama   Well, we're glad today is the audition. Gives you a chance to take a break from spreading rumors about us all over school.

Paulina   Me?! Whatever.

Mercy *and* **Gifty**   Yeah, you!

Mercy   Spreading rumors!

Gifty   And rumors hurt!

Paulina   Please. I have better things to do.

Ama   Then why did you start telling everyone in our dormitory *again* that I'm not a virgin?! You *know* that's not true!

Paulina   I don't know what you do to keep Osei.

Gifty   Or that I'm cheating in English class?

Paulina   Everyone knows you can't read, Gifty!

Gifty   I'm getting better!

Mercy   Or telling everyone that I'm lying about my father being a doctor!

Paulina   Why else would he let you dress like you're from the bush?!

Ama   Well, at least she knows who her father is.

Mercy *and* **Gifty**   Yeah!

Paulina   Excuse me?

Ama   Tell me, has your mother figured it out yet? Or is she still busy spreading her legs for every man in your village?

Paulina   Wow, Ama?! After all I have done for you.

Ama   All you've done?! You talk about all of us like we're dogs! I'm supposed to be your best friend and look at what you say about me, my family, and my boyfriend!

Paulina   He's trash, Ama.

Ama   At least he is real!

Paulina   What?

Ama   Everyone with half a brain can figure out that you have been making Kofi up!

Paulina   No I haven't!

Ama   He never calls for you.

Mercy   Never!

Ama   Never shows up to the dances

Gifty   Never!

Ama   And I don't know how you get these letters he alledgedly sends.

I work in the mail room and I've never seen a letter come for you even once! They all just magically appear!

Mercy *and* **Gifty**   Magic!

Paulina   I have *always* known you were jealous of me, Ama!

Ama   Of what?!

Paulina   Everything! You want to dress like me, act like me, be me!

Ama   You don't even want to be yourself!

Paulina   Yeah, okay.

Ama   Tell me . . . How many times did Headmistress have to send you to hospital in our first year, eh? Your face full of blisters and blood from all the bleaching cream you would use!

Mercy   What?   **Gifty**   Bleaching cream?!

Paulina   Ama . . . You promised—

Ama   —No! I'm done covering for you! Everyone should know the truth, Paulina!

And the truth is you hate yourself so much, you would do *anything* to change!

Paulina   Well, since we're being all honest! Do the girls know that your father is in prison? That the pastor was stealing money from his own church?!

Mercy *and* **Gifty**   Whaaaaat?

Ama   You are such a—

Paulina   A what?!

Ericka   Paulina, that's enough!

Paulina   Oh, you don't want me to get started on you, Ericka!

Ericka   You need to relax, okay?!

Paulina   And you need to stay out of my way! I will take you down too!

Ericka   Oh yeah?

Paulina   Yeah! So don't fuck with me, sweetie!

The girls hear **Headmistress Francis** *coming down the hall.*

All Girls   Eh-eh! / She's coming! / She's here! / I'm so nervous.

Headmistress Francis *and* **Eloise** *enter the cafeteria. The girls play nice for them.*

Headmistress Francis   Oh my goodness! Look at how lovely you girls look!

All Girls   Thank you Headmistress.

Headmistress Francis   Girls, I would like to introduce you to Ms. Eloise Amponsah—former Miss Ghana 1966. She is one of the recruiters for this year's pageant.

Eloise   Good afternoon, ladies. It is such a pleasure to meet you all.

All Girls   Thank you, Ms. Amponsah.

Paulina   Yes! It is very nice to see you again.

Eloise (*dismissive*)   Yes.

Headmistress Francis   Right, you remember Paulina. And this here is Ama.

Ama   Hello.

Headmistress Francis   Mercy and Gifty.

Mercy   Good afternoon.

Gifty   We are happy to receive you.

Headmistress Francis   Our shy little Nana here.

Nana   Hello, ma'am.

Eloise   Ma'am? Oh please, save that for my mother.

And Headmistress, who is this lovely young lady? What is your name?

Ericka   Ericka Boafo.

Headmistress Francis   She just recently transferred into the school from the States.

Eloise   America?! Wow.

Ericka   Yes, but I have returned to Ghana now to complete my studies here, in my home country.

Paulina *laughs.*

Headmistress Francis   Paulina.

Paulina   Sorry. She just made me think of . . . sorry, it's nothing. My apologies.

Headmistress Francis   Now, as I told you, Eloise, the girls picked this song themselves and have been working on it all week in preparation for this audition.

Eloise   Lovely.

Headmistress Francis   Now, Ericka here hasn't had time to rehearse with us but she says she knows the song very well.

(*To* **Ericka**.) So just do the best you can, okay?

Ericka   I will.

Headmistress Francis   Great! Ms. Amponsah, please have a seat here.

Eloise   Thank you.

Headmistress Francis   Okay now, let's get into formation here and when I point to you, step out to sing your part. Ama—why don't we start with you.

The girls all stand in formation with **Ama** *up center.*

Headmistress Francis   Now, straight backs, chests up, and just let the music float out of you. Here we go.

She blows the note into her pitch pipe and cues the girls. They all sing a unison "Oooo" a cappella. (It's "The Greatest Love of All.")

Ama (*earnest*)

I believe de children are de future.
Teach dem well and let dem lead the way.
Show dem all de beauty they possess inside.

Headmistress Francis   Nana.

Nana (*barely audible*)

Give dem a sense of pride to make it easier,
let de children's laughter remind us how we used to be.

Headmistress Francis   Gifty.

Gifty *steps up smiling with confidence.*

Gifty (*not good but very confident*)

Everybody's searching for a hero,
People need someone to look up to.
I never found anyone who fulfilled that need.

Headmistress Francis   Get ready, Mercy. You are next.

Gifty

A lonely place to be.
So I learned to depend on me.

Mercy (*too high pitched*)

I decided long ago
Never to walk in anyone's shadow.

Headmistress Francis   Eh-eh, Mercy! Just bring your key down.

Mercy (*too low*)

If I fail, if I succeed,
At least I'll live as I believe.
No matter what they take from me,
They can't take away my dignity.

Headmistress Francis (*another blow into the pitch pipe*)   Okay, everyone.

All Girls

Because the greatest love of all is happening to me.
I found the greatest love of all inside of me.

Headmistress Francis   Okay, Paulina's next . . .

Paulina *steps to the front, full of all the confidence she can muster.*

Paulina (*it's lovely*)

I believe the children are our future.
Teach them well and let them lead the way.
Show them all the beauty they possess inside.

Headmistress Francis   Ericka, you're next, dear.

Paulina (*more confident*)

Give them a sense of pride to make it easier.
Let the children's laughter remind us how we used to be.

Ericka *steps in front of* **Paulina**.

Ericka (*channeling Whitney—her voice is amazing*)

I decided long ago,
never to walk in anyone's shadow.
If I fail,
If I succeed
At least I'll live as I believe. No matter what they take from me.
They can't take away my dignity.

Eloise (*inspired!*)   Praise God!

All Girls   because the
greatest love of all
is happening to me. I
found the greatest
love of all inside of me.

Ericka (*ad libbing and riffing
to her heart's content*)

All of the girls, except **Paulina**, *start to clap, cheer, and praise*
Ericka. **Paulina** *begins to hyperventilate—she's about to explode.*

Eloise   Bravo! Ericka! You are quite a talent! You would make
quite the splash at the Miss Ghana pageant!

The girls all cheer for **Ericka** *again, then—*

Paulina   NOOOOOOO!

Headmistress Francis   Eh-eh! Paulina. Calm yourself!

Paulina   NO! SHE CAN'T BE THE NEXT MISS GHANA
BECAUSE SHE IS NOT EVEN A REAL GHANAIAN!

Mercy   You say what?   **Gifty**   Eh-eh! How?

Paulina   She was born in America! Her mother is white!
Ericka Johnson!

Ericka   What?!

Paulina   Boafo isn't even her real name!

Mercy *and* **Gifty**   Woooooow!

Headmistress Francis   Paulina!

Paulina   It's in her file!

Headmistress Francis   Her file?!

Paulina   She's a bastard! Her father only claimed her now because her mother is dead!

Headmistress Francis   I can't believe this!

Ericka   Who the hell do you think you are?!

Paulina   I said to not mess with me, didn't I?!

Headmistress Francis   Hey! Girls, stop this!

Ama   This is a new low / even for you, Paulina!

Ericka   —That is none of your business!

Paulina   No one wants you here! Not even your own father!

Headmistress Francis   Paulina, enough!

Paulina   Why are you yelling at me? Nana gave me her file!

Headmistress Francis   What?!

Ama   Nana!

Headmistress Francis   Is that true?

Nana   I can explain, Headmistress.

Paulina   And that's not the first time!

Nana   No, I only did it for you!

Paulina   Was that before or after you erased all of your detention marks?

Headmistress Francis   Excuse me?!

Nana   That is not true / Headmistress!

Paulina   —It is true! She said you were trying to keep her from getting into college!

Headmistress Francis   Unbelievable! This is unbelievable!

Something is going on with **Paulina**'*s face.*

Eloise   Franny, I don't know what's going on, but can I just pick someone and skedaddle—

Paulina   Well, it can't be Ericka! The rules clearly state that you have to be BORN IN GHANA to REAL GHANAIAN parents! No knockoffs!

Eloise   Knockoffs?!

Paulina *is now fully concerned with what is going on with her face. It's burning or bleeding or something. She continues to try to cover it.*

Ericka   You are so disgusting, Paulina! Everything everyone says / about you is true!

Ama   —You are so crazy and desperate / Paulina!

Mercy   This is why we didn't borrow your dresses!

Gifty   You are crazy and desperate!

Eloise   Ericka . . . Is this true?

Ericka   Well . . .

Beat.

Ama   It's probably another lie! That's all Paulina does!

Mercy *and* **Gifty**   Spread rumors and lies!

Headmistress Francis   Paulina . . .

Paulina*'s face is now blistering and bleeding.*

Mercy   Eh-eh, is that blood?

Gifty   Blood?!

Eloise   —Yes, what is going on there?

Headmistress Francis   Ama get me a bowl of cold water and a washcloth. Now!

Nana   —You wish you looked like Ericka!

Paulina   Shut up, Nana!

Nana   NO! You shut up, Paulina!

She walks up to **Paulina** *and snatches the cream from her dress.*

Paulina   Give me that!

Mercy *and* **Gifty**   Eh-eh! Bleaching cream!

Nana   I AM SO SICK OF YOUR SHIT!

Headmistress Francis   Hey. Hey! Stop it!

Mercy   Nana!

Gifty   She said "Shit!"

Ericka   CAN'T YOU SEE, PAULINA?! You're a fucking bitch! That's why everyone hates you!

Headmistress Francis   Ericka!

Paulina   And you are a half-caste bastard!

Headmistress Francis   HEY! THAT IS ENOUGH! . . . I CANNOT BELIEVE THIS! This is absolutely REPREHENSIBLE behavior! You should all be ashamed of yourselves!

All Girls (*eventually*)   Sorry, Headmistress.

Headmistress Francis   Eloise, I assure you this is far and beyond their usual characters.

Eloise   I would hope so.

Headmistress Francis   Can you please step out for a moment? I need to deal with all of this.

Eloise   . . . Sure.

She shakes her head, mainly at **Ericka**, *and walks off.*

Headmistress Francis   Paulina and Ericka, you two sit down. And the rest of you—report straight to your dormitories. And be prepared because *all* of you will be receiving several detentions for your actions today!

All Girls   Yes, Headmistress.

The girls start to exit. **Nana** *walks over to* **Headmistress Francis** *and hands her the container of bleaching cream.*

Nana   Should I give this to you?

Headmistress Francis   Uh, yes, I'll take it, Nana. Now go.

Nana *exits. All of the girls are gone.* **Headmistress Francis** *stares at the container and then puts it on the table between* **Paulina** *and* **Ericka**.

Headmistress Francis   I mean, I don't even know where to begin with this. Of all the years I have been headmistress of this school, I have never seen anything like this.

Stealing files! Foul language! Fighting! All of which are grounds for expulsion!

Ericka   I didn't do—   **Paulina**   Headmistress, she was—

Headmistress Francis   Eh-eh! I did not ask either of you to speak!

Have I not gone above and beyond for you girls? Eh?

Paulina—I have looked after you like you are my own child. Took care of you and paid for things your mother couldn't afford. And let's not talk about the countless hospital bills I incurred only for you to turn around and start using this mess again?

And you, Ericka. I know this has been a very tough time for you, but fighting is not the way to deal with these feelings—

Ericka   Headmistress—   **Paulina**   Look, she was the one—

Headmistress Francis   I am not finished!

Now . . . while you two are students at my school, your studies will be your number one and *only* priority! Understand?

Ericka *and* **Paulina** *nod.*

Headmistress Francis   Now, I'm going to go find Eloise and when I come back, you two better have fixed this or no one is going to the pageant. Do I make myself clear?

Paulina   Yes, Headmistress.   **Ericka**   Yes, Headmistress.

Headmistress Francis   Good.

She exits. **Paulina** *and* **Ericka** *sit in silence for a long beat.*

Paulina *bursts into tears.* **Ericka** *turns away and perhaps some tears are shed too.*

Ericka   You crossed the line!

Paulina   Well, I'm not sorry! Ms. Amponsah should know the truth. It is against the rules.

Ericka   Please! This isn't about the pageant!

Paulina   It's the truth!

Ericka   If you don't like me, fine! But you had no right to—

Paulina   —You stole all of my friends!

Ericka   That's how you treat your friends?

Paulina   You came in here, acting like you've got everything

Ericka   —Lotion and makeup?!—

Paulina   —Like you didn't have a care in the world!

Ericka   Listen you don't know SHIT about my life okay?!—

Paulina   —Oh really?—

Ericka   —NOTHING! I wasn't rich. I didn't have friends.

Paulina   Whatever.

Ericka   You think those white kids wanted anything to do with me? You think there were any other Black kids in Portsmouth?! I was always alone! . . . And my father . . . was here. With his cocoa factory . . . And his wife and children.

Living this perfect life . . . Not even thinking about me. . . Ashamed of me . . . His white daughter.

Paulina   Oh please.

Ericka   And you think my life was easy? My mother is all I had
. . . And you try watching your mother die and talk to me about
how easy that is . . .

Did you ever stop to think that I might be jealous of you?!

Paulina *sucks teeth loudly.*

Ericka   That you know where you come from? . . . That you have
a family?

I'm sorry that you don't see how lucky you are.

Paulina   Lucky? Are you serious? Lucky where?! That my
mother has eight children, most of us with different fathers?
Lucky that we are the poorest people in our village? Lucky to be
the darkest one in my family? That even with our little bit of
money, my mother gave me bleaching cream instead of food—
cause that would "serve me better in life?!" . . . That's not
luck, Ericka, okay?! The only luck I had was getting a scholarship
to Aburi.

Small beat.

And you . . . You're the daughter of one of the richest men in the
country. You will always have something . . . Always . . .

Small beat.

. . . Trust me—my mother would have gladly traded me in for you
. . . Clearly . . . She was right.

Ericka   No she wasn't.

Paulina   Yes, she was . . . Listen, the world has already decided
. . . You are better than me.

Ericka   That's not true.

Paulina   Ericka . . . Yes it is.

They sit in silence.

After a moment, **Headmistress Francis** *and* **Eloise** *enter
the cafeteria.*

Headmistress Francis   I'm back, girls. And I believe you have something to say to Ms. Amponsah?

Paulina   Yes. We are very sorry for our behavior, Ms. Amponsah.

Ericka   Yes, very sorry. This will never happen again.

Eloise   Thank you. But trust me, I understand how heated things can get when it comes to competition. After all, I am Miss Ghana 1966 and I did not get that prestigious title without getting a bit of dirt on my hands.

Headmistress Francis   Now, I've already asked Ms. Amponsah if she would like to come back another day to make a decision, but—

Eloise   Oh no, no, no. This is time sensitive.

Headmistress Francis   Right.

Eloise   Now, besides that "episode," you have a lovely group of girls, but it's clear the standouts are certainly Paulina and Ericka here. Though in light of what Paulina has discovered, Ericka would be disqualified if the MGU committee found out.

Headmistress Francis   Yes, I understand.

Eloise   . . . And that is why we are not going to tell them.

Paulina   What?

Ericka   . . . What?

Headmistress Francis   Eloise, now wait just a minute here. You can't do that.

Eloise   Oh, I can . . . and I will.

Beat.

Headmistress Francis   Well, I won't allow it! I will call the MGU committee myself if I have to.

Eloise   Listen, I don't have time for this! I've got a pageant I need to win.

Headmistress Francis   But . . . like this?

Eloise   Well, you can't get anywhere in this world by playing fair.

Headmistress Francis   So you would ruin these girls' dreams because of something this stupid?!

Eloise   Yes, because I want to win!

Headmistress Francis   But you won! Eloise, they named *you* Miss Ghana!

Eloise   Yes, and once I left Ghana, no one cared! Those MGU judges didn't even blink my way! I might as well have been invisible! So if I have to push every darkie out of the way, so be it! I want my damn promotion! I want, for once in my life, to *finally* be seen!

Composes herself.

And anyway, I'm not the only person who will benefit here.

If Ericka wins Miss Ghana, she gets the crown, Aburi gets a generous donation, and Ghana will *finally* get some real recognition on a global platform. How is that not a win—win for everyone?!

Headmistress Francis   It's not for Paulina—

Eloise   Oh who cares about—(*remembers—then sweetly*)   Listen, Paulina . . . dear. You are a beautiful and bright young lady. And I think you would make a fine candidate for the Miss Ghana pageant . . . Next year.

Paulina (*trying to control her tears*)   Okay.

Eloise   I can't make any promises on whether you'll be selected, but I am Miss Ghana 1966 and my recommendation will hold some weight.

Paulina   Okay.

Eloise   But . . . I can't speak for what I will do if you don't keep that mouth of yours shut about all of this . . . Do you understand?

Paulina (*eventually*)   Yes.

Eloise   Good . . . Do we all have an understanding?

Ericka   Yeah.

Headmistress Francis (*eventually*)   Yes.

Eloise (*re:* **Ericka**)   Good. Now . . . I can't wait to show the recruiting team the diamond that I found in this mine!

(*To* **Paulina**.) Just you wait, Paulina. You will see all of the doors that Ericka is going to open for you! She is going to put Ghana on the map! You'll be thanking her—trust me!

(*Back to* **Ericka**.) Now, dear, let's talk about dresses . . .

Ericka *and* **Eloise** *walk off. After a moment,* **Headmistress Francis** *sits down next to* **Paulina**. **Paulina** *begins to sob as* **Headmistress Francis** *pulls her into an embrace.*

Epilogue

Mercy *and* **Gifty** *sit at the cafeteria table.*

Mercy   Really good. Now let's—

Gifty   Can we hurry up? It's almost time for the pageant!

Mercy   I know, but let's just read these next sentences and then we'll be done.

Gifty (*sighs*)   Okay.

(*Reads.*) "I love writing you letters from my new debroom"

Mercy   Bedroom.

Gifty   "Bedroom . . . You should see my new deb."

Mercy   Bed.

Gifty   "Bed. It is my favorite color . . . purple."

Mercy   Really, really good, Gifty.

Gifty   Thank you.

Mercy   You see? You just had to take your time with it.

Gifty   Yeah . . . Writers, man. They really know their stuff.

Mercy   You know, now that Headmistress is having that library built on campus, we should ask her for more books like this.

Gifty   Yeah . . . Books. Anyway, where is everyone? This is the MISS GLOBAL UNIVERSE PAGEANT!

Mercy   I know.

Gifty   And Headmistress promised that we could watch it after last period!

Mercy   I'm sure Headmistress is on her way, Gifty.

Gifty   This anxiety is too much, oh!

Nana *walks into the cafeteria. She sits at the table.*

Mercy *and* **Gifty**   Nana! / Hey! / We haven't seen you in forever!

Nana   Hey, girls.

Mercy   Finally off detentions.

Nana   I know. Finally done.

Gifty   We thought we'd never see you again!

Mercy   I can't imagine. Being on detentions for two whole months—

Gifty   —Sixty days—

Mercy   —No food.

Nana   —I had food.

Gifty   —No water

Nana   —It wasn't a dungeon you guys.

Mercy   —It basically was!

Gifty   —Basically.

Mercy   —Going from class then straight to the office to work.

Gifty   —Eating lunch—

Mercy   —With Headmistress just watching over you like

Both **Mercy** *and* **Gifty** *impersonate what they think the stare was like.*

Nana   You guys are so silly.

Mercy   Glad that Headmistress saw that we weren't involved in all of that.

Gifty   I don't know if my spirit could take two months of detentions.

Nana   I'm just glad it's over.

Mercy   Yeah . . . Anyway, it feels like we have so much to catch up on. What's going on with you?

Nana   Well—

Mercy   Ooh! So I was able to convince my dad to let me and Gifty stay here.

Gifty (*touched*)   Uncle James is the best.

Mercy   After "Audition Day" things were touch and go,

Gifty   Touch and go.

Mercy   But I had to explain to him, just sit him down and talk straight business, you know? Daughter to father.

Maybe emotional . . . but like fake emotions.

And it was hard, oh. Trying to explain to him how it is to be the child of a doctor, at one of the best schools in Ghana, trying to get good grades, look after my cousin . . .

. . . and not have new shoes . . .

Gifty   . . . So hard . . .

Mercy   But I promised him that Gifty and I would stay out of trouble and get good grades for the rest of year. *And*! He said if we do that, he *might* get me and Gifty . . . you're not going to believe this, Nana . . .

Nana   What?

Mercy   A new pair of Nikes!

Mercy *and* **Gifty** *celebrate.*

Gifty   Can you believe it?!

Mercy   I can already feel how good they will be on my feet.

Gifty   So good.

Nana   That's amazing. Congrats.

Mercy   Oh! And Gifty is reading now! And she's pretty good too. She just finished her first book.

Nana   Really?!

Gifty   Yes! *James and the Giant Peach*. Really powerful stuff.

Nana   Good for you.

Mercy   Anyway, enough about us, what's been up with you, Nana?

Nana (*kind of proud*)   Well, Headmistress is letting me join the football team next week. I'm going to be playing goalie. I'm really excited about it.

Mercy   That's nice.

Gifty   Good for you, Nana.

Nana   Thanks. Headmistress thinks some extracurriculars will help with my college applications.

Gifty   Speaking of—where is Headmistress?! The pageant!

Mercy   I'm sure she's coming, Gifty, relax.

Ama *walks into the cafeteria and comes to sit with the girls. Perhaps* **Gifty** *gets excited that it's* **Headmistress Francis***, but is deflated when she sees* **Ama***.*

Ama   Nana. Finally free, eh?! Welcome back.

Nana   Thanks. It's good to be out again.

Ama   I'm sure.

Nana   I heard you got a few detentions too.

Ama   I did. Only for a week though. Which was fine. Working in the mail room is the worst. If I never have to see another envelope again for the rest of my life, I'll be okay.

The girls all giggle.

Mercy   Ama! Aren't you going to tell Nana the good news?

Gifty   Hello!

Ama   Oh yeah, I got accepted to University of Ghana—early decision!

Nana   Wow, Ama! That's amazing. Congratulations!

Ama   Thanks. I am still waiting to hear from the schools I applied to in America, but I'm really excited about U of G.

Mercy   Umm, Ama, that is not the news we were talking about!

Gifty   Yeah. Who cares about college?

Ama   What?

Mercy (*holds up left hand*) Uhh . . . hello!	**Gifty** (*holds up left hand*) Uhh . . . hello!

Ama   Oh, I mean, it's not even a big deal.

Mercy Excuse me, yes it is!	**Gifty** Eh-eh! It's very big, oh!

Ama   But Osei told me that he wanted to make things official and. . . he proposed!

Mercy Ahhhh!	**Gifty** Ahhhh!

Ama (*calming them down*)   It was supposed to be a secret, you guys! We said we'd wait to share the news with our friends until after we told our parents. So we're not official yet.

Mercy   You might as well be!

Gifty   And you better claim him.

Mercy   Because if you don't—

Gifty   We will!

The girls all laugh.

They settle. **Gifty** *looks out of the cafeteria. Small beat.*

Nana   So . . . has anyone seen Paulina?

Ama   Not really. Just in class.

Mercy   I heard that she is still really sad.

Gifty   Very depressed.

Nana   I've barely seen her. Especially since she had to move dormitories.

Mercy   And to the scary dormitory too.

Gifty   I heard Headmistress only puts delinquents in there.

Mercy   I heard she's barely eaten anything.

Gifty   And it takes her a long time to get out of bed.

Ama   It's probably best that she's not around people. Maybe she's learned something.

Nana   You know, she wrote me a letter. Slipped it under my door.

Mercy   She wrote you one too?

Gifty   Us too.

Ama   I'm sure Headmistress forced her to.

Nana   I can't believe she lied about all of that.

Mercy   Who would make up a story like that?

Gifty   And so detailed.

Mercy   Right. That Ericka is not Ghanaian? White mother?

Gifty   That is too much.

Nana   Did you write her back?

Mercy   Eh, I thought about it.

Gifty   Thought.

Mercy   But I didn't.

Gifty   Yeah, no.

Mercy   Still . . . I've decided to forgive her.

Gifty   Clearly, she lost her mind.

Nana You think she'll come out and watch today?

Gifty Well, she didn't watch the Miss Ghana pageant.

Mercy Who can blame her?

Gifty True.

Ama You think Ericka will actually win the Miss Global Universe pageant?

Nana You never know. I still think she's the best Miss Ghana we have ever had.

Mercy Yeah, she will *at least* make the top ten.

Gifty Top ten for sure.

Paulina, *dressed in her school uniform but cloaked in a black shawl and sunglasses, enters the cafeteria.*

Mercy Paulina! How are you?

Gifty Yeah. How's your heart?

Mercy Are you okay?

Gifty Do you need something?

Paulina Ladies, please. I am fine. It's just nice to be out in the fresh air again.

Mercy *and* **Gifty** Yeah / Of course / Sure, fresh air.

Paulina This has been a really difficult time on my spirit, you know? And I have done a lot of self-reflection ever since the Pageant. And I know God is working on me. With his grace, I will get through this.

Mercy *and* **Gifty** Amen.

Paulina (*notices* **Nana** *and* **Ama**) Nana . . . Ama.

Nana *and* **Ama** Mmmm.

Paulina You . . . uh. . . got my letter, yes?

Ama I did.   **Nana** Yeah.

Paulina   And . . . I know that we may never be friends again—

Ama   Nope.   **Nana**   Probably not.

Paulina   Which is fine . . . Just know . . . that I'm sorry, okay?

Ama   Whatever.

Nana   Yeah, okay.

Beat. They aren't quite sure what to do.

Mercy   Well, we're glad to see you, Paulina. We didn't know if you were going to come and watch.

Gifty   Maybe you'd be too upset.

Paulina   No, it's fine. Ericka won Miss Ghana. Good for her.

Headmistress Francis *enters the cafeteria wheeling on a TV cart.*

Headmistress Francis   Girls! Can I get a bit of help here.

All Girls (*cheering, maybe except* **Paulina**)   Headmistress! / It's time! It's time! / We can't wait!

Headmistress Francis   Well, good afternoon, girls. Yes, I know you are all very excited.

All Girls (*maybe except* **Paulina**)   YES!

Mercy (*setting up the TV*)   Gifty! Get the cord. Eh-eh—don't tangle it.

Gifty   I'm not! Just plug it in, oh.

Mercy *and* **Gifty** *continue to fuss about the plug, the TV, the pageant, etc.*

Ama   Nana, help me move this.

Nana   Okay. Ah, this is so exciting.

Ama   I know! Oh, don't forget the popcorn.

Nana   Got it!

Headmistress Francis   What a day, eh? To see one of our very own Aburi School girls—on international television.

Gifty *cannot contain her excitement.*

Mercy   Oh my goodness! What if she wins?!

Ama   That would be amazing!

Gifty   I know!

She is losing it! All the girls, except **Paulina***, applaud.* **Paulina** *smiles.*

Headmistress Francis   Okay, are we all set up now?

All Girls (*overexcited!*)   Yes!

Headmistress Francis *turns on the television and turns up the volume. The girls all watch intently.*

Ghanaian Television Announcer   And now, Ghana News Network takes you back to the Miss Global Universe pageant broadcasting live from Orlando, Florida.

The girls all cheer. Maybe not **Paulina***.*

American TV Host   Good evening, ladies and gentlemen, and welcome back to the Miss Global Universe pageant!

We have people tuning in from all over the world tonight, isn't that exciting?

All Girls   Yes!

American TV Host   But not as exciting as announcing our top ten semi-finalists!

All Girls   Ahhh!

Mercy   They're already at the top ten!

Gifty   I'm going to pass out!

Mercy   Do you see Ericka?

Gifty   There's so many girls.

Ama   Shhh!

American TV Host   Our celebrity panel judged each young lady for poise and grace while they wore an evening gown of their own choice.

Ama   I wonder which designer Ericka wore?

Mercy   You think she knows Calvin Klein?!

Gifty   Oh for sure!

Ama   Shhh!

American TV Host   Each judge personally interviewed each of our contestants with the aid of an interpreter when needed.

Ama   Interpreter?

Nana   Like they found someone who speaks Twi?

Mercy *and* **Gifty**   Yeah, right.

American TV Host   Now all of these scores will determine who will be our ten semi-finalists. As you can see, I've been joined here on stage by all of our contestants.

Mercy   How many Africans do you see?

Gifty   Eh-eh! There's too many girls! And you know I can't count that fast!

Ama   Shhhh!

Gifty (*to* **Ama**)   You need to relax!

American TV Host   Now let me remind you folks at home that these names will be read in no particular order and the competition scores will *only* be shown to you at home.

All Girls   Exclusives! / Ehhh! / Us! Only us!

American TV Host   Here now are the names of our ten semi-finalists, all competing for the title of Miss Global Universe 1986.

All Girls (*maybe except* **Paulina**)   Yaaay! / Ahhh! / My blood pressure, oh!

American TV Host   The first name on the list is . . .
Miss Brazil.

*Applause and cheesy eighties music (this happens after each
contestant is announced).*

Ama   They gave her an 8.4!

Nana   What's the highest you can get?

Ama   Probably a 10.

American TV Host   I think the audience will like . . .
Miss France.

Mercy   Which audience?

Gifty   Cause I don't like her!

American TV Host   And let's welcome . . . Miss Italy.

Nana   Wow, she's got the lowest score so far, 8.2.

Ama   What are they even basing these scores on anyway?

Mercy *and* **Gifty**   Who knows.

American TV Host   And now, come on down. . .

Gifty   MISS GHANA!

American TV Host   Miss United States.

All Girls   Of course!

Mercy   9.0! Please!

Gifty   Yeah, please!

American TV Host   We're halfway there now with . . . Miss
South Africa.

All Girls   Yaaay! / Wooo! / Finally! Someone from Africa!

Nana   Oh wait . . . you guys, she's a white.

All Girls   Again?! / These people! / Of course she is!

American TV Host   And here comes Miss Switzerland.

Mercy   8.3?! With that crazy hair?!

Gifty   Two words: Hot. Comb!

Headmistress Francis   Gifty.

Gifty (*under breath*)   It's true.

American TV Host   Next is Miss Venezuela!

All Girls   She's pretty. / Not bad. / Her hair is better than that other one at least. / That dress! Wow!

American TV Host   Number 8 on the list of semi-finalists is . . . Miss Greece!

Nana   Hey! There's Ericka!

All Girls (*except* **Paulina**)   Ahhh! / Ericka is on television! / I can't believe it! / Oh my God! / She looks amazing!

Headmistress Francis   Girls, please. You're going to miss the last two countries.

Mercy   One of them better be Ghana!

Gifty   Because Miss Greece looks crazy!

American TV Host   Now, ladies and gentlemen, we have two names to go and one of those names is . . . Miss Colombia.

Nana   Colombia?!

Gifty   Where is that?

Ama   South America. You need to pay attention in geography, Gifty.

Gifty   SHHH!

American TV Host   And now number 10, the last contestant who has a chance to become Miss Global Universe . . .

All Girls (*except* **Paulina**—*scattered whispers*)   Ghana / Say Ghana / If it's not Ghana, I will scream.

American TV Host   She is . . . Miss Sweden!

Everyone is stunned silent.

Up next—the evening gown competition featuring a performance by R&B star Bobby Brown!

Light applause and music is heard on the television. **Headmistress Francis** *lowers the volume on the television.*

Silence.

Headmistress Francis   Wow.

Paulina   Wow.

Mercy   I can't believe it.

Paulina   Yeah.

Gifty   Maybe it's a mistake.

Nana   Ericka looked pretty though.

Ama   Not pretty enough.

Silence.

Headmistress Francis   Girls, I know you are disappointed . . . I am too. But look at the bright side—you got see one of your own classmates on television, representing our country.

That is a very big deal. And who knows, maybe next year things will be different.

Paulina   Yeah . . .

Ama   Maybe.

Gifty   I guess.

Mercy   So . . . all of that? For what?

Nana   All for nothing?

Paulina   All for nothing.

She turns up the volume on the television.

American TV Host   And we're back, folks, with the top ten most beautiful women in the world!

Thunderous applause from the television. It becomes louder and louder and louder as the girls watch in silence. Lights fade.

End of play.